# ROCK MY
# WEDDING
## YOUR DAY YOUR WAY

# CHARLOTTE O'SHEA

# ROCK MY
# WEDDING
## YOUR DAY YOUR WAY

EBURY
PRESS

1 3 5 7 9 10 8 6 4 2

Ebury Press, an imprint of Ebury Publishing,
20 Vauxhall Bridge Road,
London SW1V 2SA

Ebury Press is part of the Penguin Random House group of companies
whose addresses can be found at global.penguinrandomhouse.com

 Penguin
Random House
UK

First published by Ebury Press in 2017

www.eburypublishing.co.uk

A CIP catalogue record for this book is available from the British Library

**Editor:** Lydia Good
**Design:** Jim Smith Design Ltd
For photo credits please see pages 214–215

ISBN 9781785033537

Printed and bound in China by Toppan Leefung

Penguin Random House is committed to a sustainable future for our
business, our readers and our planet. This book is made from Forest
Stewardship Council® certified paper.

**For my Mabel**
Sunshine girl, may your life be forever
filled with joy, love and happiness.

# Contents

# Introduction

An adventure. That's what you are about to embark on. A magical love-fuelled journey towards what will be one of the best days of your lives. It thrills me to the core that via the advice and inspirational styling ideas within this book we have the opportunity to be a part of your wedding. Truly.

Your wedding day is the one occasion that can bring those closest and dearest to you together to celebrate yours and your partner's commitment to marriage. We completely understand how important it is for that occasion to wow from an aesthetic perspective, run smoothly from a practical perspective, and for both of you to really, *really* enjoy it. We appreciate nothing more than when we feature a real wedding on the blog (rockmywedding. co.uk) where, aside from the froth and the fancy, the couple simply had a fantastically brilliant time from start to finish.

It's about the pretty, it's about the party, but most of all? It's about the joy.

We sincerely hope that this book and its carefully curated contents bring you hours and hours of exactly that. Read from cover to cover, or dip in and out as and when you please; we're delighted to be accompanying you on this crazy, beautiful, life-changing ride.

**Charlotte O'Shea**
Founder of rockmywedding.co.uk

# Your Unique Style

The first question that presents itself when embarking on planning one of the most significant days of your lives to date tends to be: But where do we begin in creating a wedding that is truly unique? Quite. Where do you begin?

It is so very easy to drown in the detail. I should know – I've been there, seen it, done it, got the proverbial T-shirt, as it were. And then I simply took a step back and started over.

I really don't want you to have to start over, I want you to make considered, thoroughly personal choices when it comes to your sartorial and décor style. 'Personal' being the operative word here; your wedding should be a reflection of you both as a couple, be that simplistic and classic, minimalistic and chic, romantic and rustic or dancing on the tables until dawn and everything in between. It's about creating the kind of wedding day that is undeniably yours.

I always suggest starting with the things that you love. Reflect on the best memories you have experienced together – a wonderful holiday, your favourite music, dining al fresco in the summer months, or winter evenings spent in front of the fire with a bottle of wine. There will be a common thread that unfolds, I promise. So, start there.

You should also consider the interior of your home, as there is usually a colour scheme that occurs more frequently than others, and a type of furniture that you prefer – vintage and up-cycled, sleek and modern, statement and bold. Take these elements and consider how you might utilise the general themes that emerge within your floral and stationery designs, for example. This will help you to feel yourselves on the day as it will effortlessly reflect your taste and lifestyle so that not only you, but your friends and family, will naturally recognise the look and feel of your day as being synonymous with you as a couple.

Just because you are organising a wedding doesn't mean that you have to include absolutely everything that is traditionally associated with a wedding. Not a fan of cake? Don't have one. Not particularly keen movers and shakers? Then don't feel the need to have a first dance. If it doesn't interest you then simply don't waste your time thinking about it: concentrate on the aspects that are the most fun because – guess what? – you'll experience a truly memorable and thoroughly enjoyable day. A wedding that is perfectly reflective of *you*.

CHAPTER ONE

# ORDER OF THE DAY

# The Ceremony

More often than not I hear that a couple's favourite part of their wedding was the ceremony itself. And so it should be; committing to be each other's life partner is, after all, the main purpose of the day's celebrations.

Ultimately you will be choosing to commit to marriage in either a religious ceremony at your place of worship, or in a civil ceremony at your chosen wedding venue or a register office. Should you wish to host a ceremony witnessed by your nearest and dearest in a location that isn't licensed for religious or civil ceremonies, particularly an outdoor area for example, you could opt for a humanist ceremony. Please be aware that in some countries a humanist ceremony is not recognised by law (in the UK it is only recognised in Scotland).

Although there are certain formalities to every ceremony that are required in order to legalise your marriage, for the most part you are able to personalise the event to suit your style and individuality. There is nothing quite like being a guest at a ceremony where the couple legally commit to each other complemented with readings, music and vows that are truly a reflection of them and their relationship journey.

### Vows

As mentioned above, there will be certain vows you are required to take in order to legalise your union, but that's not to say you can't write and recite your own words of wisdom and declarations of love dedicated to your partner during the proceedings. Personally penned vows and promises are *beautiful*. I'm not one for regrets as a general rule, but I do wish my now husband and I had considered writing our own. I've often been my most emotional at a wedding whilst listening to two of our friends share their hopes and dreams for their future lives together right before saying 'I do'.

Yes, that's right, I'm guaranteed to be the embarrassing teary guest with the smeary mascara at your wedding, should you choose to compose your very own romantic prose. And I shall not be apologising for it.

### Readings

Just like any other tradition, there is no rule to say you have to incorporate readings into your ceremony. From experience, there seems to be a general consensus that choosing appropriate readings for your wedding can actually be quite difficult, despite the seemingly abundant list of popular and well-loved options to choose from.

For a selection of favourites please visit rockmywedding.co.uk/readings, and if none of those is quite the right fit, how about choosing a passage from your favourite book? It doesn't have to be something well known or instantly recognisable to your guests, as long as it is meaningful to you. A heartfelt poem or lyrics from a significant song are also an option, and whomever you ask to deliver your reading will undoubtedly make considered suggestions too.

## Music

What music to play at your wedding is quite possibly *the* most personal choice of all; it's incredibly important to lots of people, myself included. My husband and I deliberated for hours on which tunes we wanted to incorporate into our ceremony; they needed to be relevant and loved by us as a couple but also appropriate to the setting. I'm all for pretty much choosing whatever you desire, but lyrics associated with loss or heartbreak probably aren't *ideal* when you are just about to officially enter into lifelong wedded bliss.

Traditionally, a piece of music is chosen for both the aisle ascent and descent – processional and recessional – as well as the signing of the register. You may also want to consider songs that your guests will stand up and join in with at certain points throughout the ceremony.

Depending on the sound system facilities available at your venue, popular tracks by your favourite artists are relatively straightforward to organise. There is also a wide variety of live performers who are experts at creating the perfect atmosphere, from pianists to choirs, to a full brass band. We chose a string quartet who not only learnt the melody to one of my favourite songs to accompany my walk up the aisle but, for little extra cost, also stayed for a few extra hours post ceremony to play a mixture of classical and pop songs whilst my friends and family enjoyed cava and canapés. It's worth asking any entertainers you hire what their hourly rate is in addition to the standard pricing – drinks on the lawn in the sunshine with the sound of strings in the background was a really wonderful addition to our wedding day.

# The Reception

**After the wedding breakfast plates have been cleared away and everyone has laughed their socks off at the speeches, your reception festivities can really begin.**

## Music

Traditionally, a reception revolves around the dance floor, with couples choosing musical accompaniment in order for their guests to let their hair down and throw some (sometimes fairly unusual) shapes. What to choose really comes down to the music that you love to listen to, and of course your budget. In terms of live bands, there is a wealth of genres available, from funky soul to rhythm and blues, to rock 'n' roll. And of course brilliant tribute or cover bands who will undoubtedly perform their most heartfelt versions of the ultimate popular party classics.

Bands vary in price dramatically, and the most common increase in expense usually stems from the number of members in your chosen group. The more musicians involved, the higher the price tag. In comparison to a DJ, bands tend to play sets rather than continuously, so please do ask how long each set is expected to be and if the band will offer their speakers and equipment for a playlist of your choosing in the interim.

A DJ is a great option for ensuring a wide variety of songs, genres and eras is covered. They should be able to make suggestions on tried-and-tested dance floor fillers, as well as accepting requests for your must-have tunes.

You and your partner may wish to kick off the evening musical entertainment with a 'first dance', which can either be arranged with your band and/or DJ to announce your presence on the dance floor, or with a member of staff at your venue. Couples often choose a song that is important to them in some way and holds some sentimental value. Others prefer a more casual approach and are happier with a universally appealing tune, encouraging their guests to join them on the dance floor straight away to really get the party started. If you don't fancy an all-eyes-on-you scenario, there's nothing like a conga line or an eighties anthem to get everyone involved! As their first dance, friends of ours choreographed an entire routine to a hip-hop track that was completely unexpected. It was utterly brilliant. And, so I was told, took quite a lot of time investment and preparation. It was completely worth it for them but, understandably, not right for everyone.

## Fun and games

Of course music isn't the only method of reception entertainment. Any kind of activity that requires guest participation is always well received and a successful ice breaker. Much-loved garden games such as giant jenga and croquet are relatively easy to set up in outdoor or larger indoor spaces. You could turn it up a notch with school sports day inspired races, such as the egg and spoon, or challenge your bridesmaids to wear a sack over their fancy frocks and see who's first to cross the finish line. Over the years I've seen photographs of many a coconut shy and a rustic welly wang, yet as a wedding guest I've never actually experienced either. And I would *love* to. So. Much. Fun.

★ DANCEFLOOR RULES ★

THE DANCEFLOOR SHOULD
ALWAYS BE OCCUPIED.

LUNGES ARE ENCOURAGED.

'DANCE OFFS' SHOULD
TAKE PLACE WHERE
APPROPRIATE.... BUT OFTEN.

ALL STYLES & TALENTS
ARE WELCOME.

GOOD DANCING SHOULD
BE APPLAUDED.

. . . . . . . . .

Photo booths are without doubt a huge hit with every generation. There is a range of companies that hire out different options, from those that produce a typical retro Polaroid strip to the more vintage-style booths that serve as an all-round experience, including props and a selection of dressing-up garments, as well as offering your friends and family special mementos.

You could also choose to create your own version of a photo booth with a relatively minimal financial outlay. Simply offering a fancy dress and prop box to your guests allows them to create their own amusing compositions and snap away as and when they please. I did exactly that and asked our professional photographer to capture the hilarity – they still remain some of my favourite moments from the day.

There is also a wealth of ideas for interactive décor that serves as guest entertainment on pages 162–163.

# Photography

If this is not the first section of the book you have dipped into then you will know that I generally offer advice from personal and professional experience that I hope you will find useful, but am more than happy for you to ignore everything I say completely and do your own thing. Besides, it wouldn't be your day, your way if it was my way, would it? Having said that, when it comes to photography, I'm going to at least attempt to be all authoritative and officious: what I lack in real-life stature I more than make up for in bossy boots. Don't say I didn't warn you!

### Where to begin

After your wedding guests have left the building and you and your partner are languishing idly in a delirious state of love, joy and happy-ever-after (and possibly champagne – I'm not judging) you will revel in the wonderful memories you have made together, surrounded by your most treasured friends and family. It's these precious memories that in time will fade, and I implore you to keep a beautiful, detailed and ultimately tangible record of them by choosing the right photographer.

I appreciate it might be tempting to employ the amateur ability of someone you know who is allegedly 'pretty good' with a camera, or appears to have the right equipment, especially if they offer to shoot your wedding for a low fee. But please, *please* research the professionals before you make any final decisions. A wedding requires a skilled and experienced photographer to capture all of those special moments. There are

no second chances – you need someone who knows exactly what to do in a wide range of indoor and outdoor environments and variable weather conditions. You also want someone you get along with, have absolute faith in to capture the day exactly how it was, and will remain unobtrusive whilst still managing to photograph all of the details, people and moments that mean the most. Like I said, wedding photography is an extremely skilled career choice.

I would begin your quest by researching photographers that are recommended by a trusted source, and you will see the work of some of our personal favourite photographers throughout this book, with specific detail on pages 184–203. We have also compiled a recommended supplier section on pages 208–213, and most if not all of these photographers will work abroad. Take the time to have an in-depth look at their portfolio, consider their use of light, the overall compositions, and whether their style of images resonates with you or not. It's important to request to see an entire wedding, not just the edited 'best bits' – you need to ensure that the photographs for the ceremony are as moving as those of the reception, as well as everything in between. I would also highly recommend that you request to view portfolios of weddings that are similar in season and location to what you have planned for your own, once you have discovered a selection of photographers that you are considering. Falling in love with the imagery from an outdoor summer wedding in the south of France, for example, is understandable,

but not at all reflective of what can be achieved if you are planning a December celebration in a Scottish castle.

All photographers, within reason, should be willing to meet with you and your partner in person once you have established they are available for your wedding date. It is wise to ask any deal-breaking questions via email if the information isn't readily available on their website, such as costs and package inclusions, prior to anyone making the effort to attend a face-to-face discussion – see page 34 for a list of these questions.

Once you have arranged your meeting, pre-prepare your queries (using our list mentioned above, if you find these helpful) for the photographer so that you are able to come away from the experience fully informed. I might be bossy, but I also genuinely want you to have the most desirable set of wedding photographs possible.

It is an added bonus if your photographer has prior experience of photographing your chosen venue, but it shouldn't be a prerequisite to your selection process; a skilled professional will be able to work with the environment with which they are presented. They should also be more than willing to arrive early at your venue if they do not have any previous knowledge of the set-up and space available, so that they can familiarise themselves with it.

## Family and group photographs

Once you have asked and received answers to all of your queries and you feel confident enough to secure your date, it's important that you give your photographer as much useful information as you can with regard to exactly which details and guests you would like photographed as a priority. I don't mean specifying the exact composition – you are paying for their creativity and expertise – but you can't expect your photographer to second guess whom you would like photographs of and with whom. It might be obvious to you, for example, that Great Aunt Maude's boyfriend is Brian, whom she met at the bingo 18 years ago, but it won't be to your photographer. It's therefore wise to advise your photographer that you would very much like a photograph of Maude and Brian together, as well as who exactly they are. It's a good idea to enlist the best man, bridesmaids or ushers to help introduce key people to your photographer on the day.

I would love to tell you that stiff, unimaginative group photographs are a thing of the past but unfortunately that isn't the case, and so all the more reason to ask to see a photographer's entire portfolio – no one wants a poker-faced wedding party all standing in a line, the result of having been asked to say 'cheese' for the 75th time. The good news is that any skilled professional worth their salt will be able to gather your favourite people together and deliver genuinely joyful and emotive results without it feeling like a chore.

## Couple's portraits

I am a big fan of the couple's portrait. HUGE. Some of the most breathtaking photographs I have ever seen are when the couple take some

time out from their day, just the two of them, and allow their photographer to capture them in all of their newly-wedded glow. I completely understand the prospect of this may seem daunting, not least if you are looking forward to the aforementioned unobtrusive and journalistic approach for the very reason you don't have to spend significant amounts of time posing rather than enjoying the festivities.

However, I promise that the right photographer will make you feel at ease and enjoy the experience, plus it's a real opportunity to take a breath and actually talk to each other about the day so far. I know my portrait session with my husband was one of the highlights of the day; admittedly some of our guests followed us around and shouted encouragement for the majority of it (!) but it was a lot of fun, and I believe the resulting photographs truly reflect that.

The right time to have a portrait session will depend on the day's schedule of events and also potentially the quality of light if you are planning on utilising the great outdoors. The light situation will depend on the season and the weather, the latter of which is almost impossible to predict until the day arrives. Your photographer will discuss with you the most preferential time they believe will offer the optimum conditions. My husband and I were married on an incredibly beautiful sunny day at the end of May, and our photographer advised the low sun in the evening would be amazing for pictures. We accepted his recommendation and took some time out before our live band played their first set at our reception.

Most photographers offer a pre-wedding shoot for their couples, which benefits both you and them in terms of getting to know each other and

becoming more comfortable in front of the camera. Do discuss this option with your photographer and any associated costs; I would heartily recommend making the effort if time and budget allow.

### Videography

The vast majority of points covered in photography are applicable also to videography, and I'm all too aware that costs can spiral and that there simply has to be a limit on spend. So, rather than dedicate a whole section to it, I would recommend that you follow the advice in our photography section, and even ask your chosen photographer for their advice, as it's brilliant when your suppliers know each other and have a smooth working relationship.

What I can tell you is that my husband and I watch our wedding film on every anniversary.

We've also watched it on Valentine's Day, on birthdays, and just on a rainy afternoon in March accompanied by a glass of wine and banoffee pie. More recently we've watched it with our daughter – I can't express how wonderful it is to re-live the day.

One of the biggest wedding supplier regrets I hear from couples is that they didn't have any of their big day recorded, which makes me very, *very* sad.

Of course, it's all about allocating your budget towards the details, events and associated supplier services that are the most important to you both. All I ask is that you research your photographer as best you can, and I can promise that having our wedding day caught in motion was one of the best decisions we made.

# Questions to ask your Photographer

### What do their fees include?

- Between what hours will you be available to photograph our wedding?
- If we require more of your time than your standard coverage, how much extra will this be per hour?
- Do you charge for travel expenses?
- How many images will we receive for your standard package?
- How much will extra images cost?
- Do we have the option of a second photographer for the day? How much extra would this cost?
- Do you offer a pre-wedding couple's/ engagement shoot? What are the charges for this?
- Are you fully insured?

### Preparation and on-the-day Activity

- There are certain group portraits we require; how should we prepare you for exactly who's who?
- We would love a couple's portrait session on the day; when would you advise is the best time for this?
- Are you familiar with our venue? If not, will you be arriving early on the day to have a look at the set-up and the available space?

### Photographs and Delivery

- Will we be provided with high-resolution files of the photographs included in our package, which we can print ourselves?
- How long after the wedding should we expect to see a preview of images?
- Will you provide an online gallery for us to browse and select our favourites from?
- How long after the wedding will you deliver the final selections of photographs?
- Does your package include an album? If not, how much extra would this be?
- Will our friends and family be able to purchase photographs via an online gallery? How much will each image cost?

CHAPTER TWO

# THE VENUE

# Choosing a Venue

Unless you have your heart set on a particular florist or photographer and will do anything to schedule your day around their availability, it is ultimately always the venue that determines the date of your wedding, and thus the ability to begin planning your big day with vigour. There isn't any one particular aspect of your wedding that I, or indeed anyone else, can tell you is the most important. But the venue, the associated décor, available space and even the configuration of that space will play a significant part in the overall organisation, styling and general flow of your day, so it is inevitably an important decision, and one that requires consideration to ensure you feel comfortable throughout the rest of the planning process.

If you have a very clear vision of how you want your wedding to look, then it may be a fairly straightforward task in terms of confirming your ideal backdrop. Perhaps you have always dreamt of a sophisticated black-tie affair in a lavish fairytale castle, a laid-back and rustic gathering within the exposed brick walls of a converted barn, or an urban warehouse celebration in big city surroundings. In which case it's simply a question of where and when, but even then there are lots of considerations to keep in mind when selecting your venue.

## Location

Many couples seek out a venue in a location that is significant to them in some way, whether it be their childhood home town, or a favourite day-trip destination. If you and your partner require a religious ceremony in your designated place of worship, you may feel your search is limited to a reception venue that doesn't require a long travel time between the ceremony and reception locations. However, I would recommend widening your scope if the location you initially assumed would offer the perfect venue simply doesn't offer the right space for the reception. Your friends and family will want to witness your special day, and will therefore be more than happy to travel to your destination of choice. One option could even be to host a 'weekend wedding', which are becoming more and more popular, with guests often staying overnight the evening before your nuptials and making a mini-break out of the occasion. And why not? It's a great excuse to extend the celebrations and a chance to catch up with all of your loved ones properly, before and after the wedding.

## Space

You may find your search is limited due to capacity, so it is definitely a good idea to begin once you have at least a general idea of the number of guests you expect, so that you don't risk falling in love with a venue, only to discover

### Ambience

If you have a very clear vision of how your day will look, then the existing interior décor features and architectural details of a venue can seem like a difficult hurdle to overcome – the often ornate and traditional décor of some stately homes, for example. However, there are plenty of venues that offer very neutral foundations for the overall backdrop – you may just need to look a little further afield and view venues that you may not have initially considered, due to distance. Alternatively, there are a myriad of ways you can work with *any* venue to make it truly your own, from florals to paper goods, and uniquely personalised and decorative projects, many of which we cover in this book. You're welcome.

Of course you might not be looking for a 'venue' at all, and are considering a back garden celebration, should the space be available to you – and even if it isn't, but if this is still your ultimate goal, there are lots of options to hire actual fields and similar outdoor areas for special occasions, so the dream can easily become a reality, as long as you're willing to be quite hands-on. Some of the loveliest and most personalised weddings I have seen are essentially a marquee in an outdoor space. Often perceived as the more traditional option, a marquee offers an almost unrivalled blank canvas for you to do exactly as you please. And if a marquee isn't quite quirky enough for your personal taste, there is a whole host of tipis, vintage-style tents and even yurts to explore, available to hire from many different companies worldwide.

you would need to cull more than half of your nearest and dearest to hold your wedding there. If you are looking to host your nuptials and your reception at the same venue, you will need to ensure that not only do they hold a civil ceremony licence, but that the capacity works for both elements of the day. Some venues, for example, offer less space for seated guests in their designated ceremony set-up than they do for the evening frivolities. Something else to watch out for is exactly where all of your guests will be seated; some venues will seat 'overflow' guests in an adjoining room or makeshift area if they do not have adequate space in the room where the ceremony is taking place.

An important factor to note for those creating their own venue: organising your event from scratch, such as hiring a marquee for a back garden wedding, doesn't necessarily mean the planning element will be easier simply because you're not restricted by rules and regulations that come with a venue. All aspects of the running of the day and supplier co-ordination will be your responsibility, unless of course you enlist the help of a freelance wedding planner.

### The planning process

The benefit of booking an established designated wedding venue is their invaluable experience and ability to assist with the majority of your requirements, from exact timings of the day's events, to the wedding breakfast menu choices, and everything in between. They will also be able to recommend trusted suppliers that they have worked with previously and who have an in-depth knowledge of the space available. Here, an important factor to note is the difference between *recommending* a supplier and *specifying* which suppliers you can or can't use. Please ensure you enquire with any venue prior to confirming the booking what their policy is with regard to using vendors that they do not have on their preferred list. With the exception of catering – whereby the venue would want to ensure they could guarantee a high standard of food preparation, delivery and service on their premises – there shouldn't be any reason why you are unable to choose exactly who *you* want to make your day as special as possible.

### The cost

In terms of budget, venue costs can vary considerably, not least depending on the number of guests you have in mind. Prices inevitably differ depending on season and day of the week. A Saturday in July, which is considered peak season, for example, will likely be more expensive than a Tuesday in January, which is considered low season. Some venues offer fairly straightforward basic packages for daily hire, including all tableware and on-the-day co-ordination, as well as certain food and drink allowances per person; there is nearly always a minimum spend requirement. This will at least give you a general gauge of the overall costs. Other venues can have what seems like anything and everything as an added extra. The best thing to do is ask – seriously – as many questions as

you feel will satisfy your understanding of the terms of the contract. And read the small print as many times as you need to in order to feel confident you are fully aware of the conditions of the agreement. Your venue is a big investment, so you need to make sure there are no hidden costs or restrictions that are going to surface when it's potentially too late to change your mind. Take it from a bride who lost her entire deposit due to an overzealous desire to secure a prime summer date, only to discover further down the line that the venue wasn't actually exclusive hire. Apparently there would be a 75th birthday complete with fancy dress and karaoke in the adjacent room to the reception, with partygoers well within their rights to use the same patio terrace area as wedding guests. Yes, that indeed happened to yours truly, and although I can laugh

at the situation now (it would have certainly made for some interesting photo opportunities) I learnt the hard way, and I really don't want you to be in the same position.

### The small print

Talking of restrictions, whilst some venues will let you dance and be merry until dawn, it's common for venues to only license their bar until around midnight. You won't automatically turn into a pumpkin as the clock strikes twelve, but you will certainly no longer be able to order a mojito. The same rules can apply for music, although there is sometimes the possibility to pay by the hour to extend the festivities beyond the confines of the standard daily hire rate.

You may also be surprised to learn that many venues have rules on throwing confetti, and some do not allow it at all, in fact. The same goes for firework displays or the lighting of candles and lanterns – the latter are sometimes allowed in designated areas only. Each venue will have various health, safety, noise and licensing regulations to abide by, and it's important that you are fully aware of any limitations before you sign on the dotted line.

We have created a detailed list of every query we can think of to present to your prospective venue, but of course, even armed with all the knowledge in the world, as with everything, there will undoubtedly be compromises. As long as you and your partner can truly envisage creating your dream day in a place that you love, that's all that really matters.

# Questions to ask your Venue

## Key questions to ask before you visit

- Is the venue exclusive use and, if not, how many events will they hold on the same day or over the same weekend?
- Do they have a licence for indoor and outdoor civil ceremonies?
- Is there a church near by?
- Do they have an alcohol licence?
- What is their capacity for:

  civil ceremony

  sit-down wedding breakfast

  party with evening guests

## Accommodation

- How many bedrooms do they have?
- Are the bedrooms included in the venue price or priced separately?
- Can our guests pay for their own accommodation at the venue, or is it up to us to foot the bill?
- Do we have to book all the on site accommodation? And are there penalties if we do not?
- Is there a good supply of local accommodation for guests, and will the venue provide help with finding it?
- Is there a bridal suite?
- Is there somewhere for the bridal party to get ready on the morning of the wedding?
- Would we have access to the gardens?
- Is there anywhere we would not be allowed to go on site?

## Pricing and payment terms

- What are the venue packages and prices? Do these change depending on the season or the day of the week?
- Are the prices quoted VAT inclusive?
- Are tables, chairs, dance floor, lighting etc. included, or is there anything shown at the venue that is not included in the hire fee?
- What are the payment terms, and is there a schedule of payment?
- Is a deposit required, and if so how much is this and when is it payable?
- What happens if we cancel our wedding?
- What protection do we have if the venue has to cancel our wedding?

## Help included in the venue hire

- Will we have a dedicated co-ordinator to help us throughout the planning process?
- Will there be a co-ordinator for the day?
- Is there a Master of Ceremonies?
- Will we get help setting up and breaking down our wedding?

### In-house catering

- How flexible are the caterers with menus? Can we have any cuisine style and menu we like or are we restricted to set menus?
- Will we be able to taste the food and see how it will be presented before our wedding? And is this included in the cost?
- Are linen, cutlery, crockery, glasses, tables, chairs and service included in the quote?
- Is VAT included in the quote?

### External catering

- Is there a list of recommended caterers we have to choose from, or can we bring in our own?
- What are the costs associated with bringing in our own caterers?

### Drink

- Does the venue have to source the drinks for us? If so, do we get these at cost price?
- Does the venue allow us to bring our own wine? If so, is there corkage charge?
- If we buy our own alcoholic and soft drinks will you chill them for us, and if so when should we deliver them?
- Does the venue have a cash bar?
- What are the bar prices? (Ask for a sample menu.)
- When can the bar be opened on the day, and when does it stop serving?

### General

- What is the latest date we can finalise and make changes to guest numbers, menus, dietary requirements and drinks orders?
- Does the venue provide a cake knife and stand?

### Civil ceremonies

- Who are the registrars who will perform the civil ceremony?
- Who books the registrars and the time of the ceremony – us or the venue?
- What is the best time to book our ceremony? (This depends on the timings of the day; what time you gain access to the venue, how long you want to get ready, what time you need. And don't forget, registrars get booked up some time in advance so check when they are free before securing your date with the venue.)

### The personal stuff

- What can we do to the venue?
- What are the limits and rules regarding decoration? (If you're planning to manage the décor yourself, or to work closely with your florist, it is worth asking the venue for a floor plan.)
- Flexibility: we want to do something very different/unique – is this possible?
- Will the venue work with our ideas or do we need to work with theirs? (Very important to get this information early on!)

### Your party

- Can we have a band?
- Are there any sound restrictions? And what time must the band/DJ stop playing?
- Does the venue have its own sound and lighting equipment?
- Is there an extra charge for evening guests?
- Is there a list of recommended suppliers?
- Can we bring in any of our own suppliers?
- Are there any particular suppliers that must be provided by the venue?
- What time can the suppliers gain access for set-up?
- Is the capacity the same throughout the entire day?

### Timings

- How long can we hire the venue for?
- What time can we check in?
- What time do we have to check out and be cleared up the next day?

### Religious ceremonies

- Please get in touch with your chosen place of worship to ask them specifically about any rules and regulations that you need to know about for your ceremony.

# Whatever the Weather

Mother Nature, she's a law unto herself, I'm afraid. Even if you book a date that is perceived as the very height of summer, no one can guarantee that the heavens will not suddenly open in the most spectacular manner on your wedding day. Alarming, admittedly, but unfortunately a very real prospect. If your ultimate goal is to host an entirely outdoorsy affair, all gentle breeze and picnics on the lawn, then this is a wonderful concept, and I truly hope it happens for you. Just make sure you have a plan B, should there be more than a few clouds in the sky.

When choosing your venue, it is wise to consider both the outside and interior space, making sure you love both and that either will ultimately work for the style of day you have in mind. Just to clarify, rain does not by any means automatically stop play, and a few showers are easy to manage. Particularly if you are organising an outdoor ceremony, I would advise hiring a selection of umbrellas so at least your guests can stay dry should there be a downpour before you get to the 'I do's'.

I know it's easier said than done, but believe me when I say some of loveliest weddings I have attended *and* featured on the blog have fallen victim to a good British soaking. It really doesn't make one iota of difference to the enjoyment of the day, I promise.

Of course there should also be consideration given to the sun putting his hat on *and* pulling out the 30°C (86°F) cigar. Take it from a bride whose May wedding was an unexpected scorcher and who wasn't prepared at all. This warm spell was most welcome in terms of canapés and cocktails in the beautiful gardens of my venue, but I was more than a little bit concerned about potential make-up meltdown, humidity-induced hair frizz, and the prospect of our guests being burnt to a crisp. As you might expect I was having such an amazing day I didn't really notice my 4pm lacklustre locks at the time, but there is significant photographic evidence. As well as my dad looking more than a little pink of cheek.

Had I been furnished with the knowledge and the experience I have now, I certainly would have been inclined to make some serious heat-proof preparations. Much like the aforementioned hire of the umbrellas, there are also companies that supply pretty parasols, thus shading your crowning glory *and* providing all sorts of *My Fair Lady*-type photo opportunities for you and your loved ones. And not forgetting the most important ingredient of all: sunscreen. Please wear some, and provide a few bottles of high SPF for your friends and family to help themselves to, should the need arise.

For the avoidance of a cosmetics calamity then please do refer to pages 102–105. I would also recommend a supply of blotting papers to combat shine. As for your hair, see pages 98–101 for a selection of inspiring styles. But the real secret is in the plait, be it a French, fishtail or full-on braided bun – any variety is a sure-fire way to keep pesky flyaways (and afternoon droop) at bay.

And when the evening becomes cooler, you can undo
your plaits to give that effortless mermaid-textured wave.
Two styles for the price of one, if you will.

Stick that in your heatwave pipe and smoke it, sunshine.

# CHAPTER THREE

# WEDDING PARTY STYLE

# Groom and Groom's Party

**Just as finding a beautiful gown is a priority for the bride, finding a suit that makes a groom look and feel confident and special on his wedding day is equally as important.**

Whether you have a specific colour scheme in mind, or desire particularly cohesive styling throughout your day, every couple should discuss their ideas of sartorial requirements, without necessarily having to reveal the final choices. Just as it's tradition – and still a very favoured one at that – for the bride to keep her dress a secret from her groom until the ceremony, some grooms may choose to do exactly the same.

I would recommend considering the suit styles and fabrics you currently love to wear, rather than feeling bound by the tradition of wearing something overtly smart and classic, such as morning suit and tails, just because it's your wedding day. On the flip side, if you've always dreamt of wearing that, and this will be your only chance, then go for it.

A three-piece tailored suit is possibly my personal favourite, as it offers such versatility in terms of a waistcoat, shirt and trousers, which will still appear elegant for the evening, once your jacket has been removed. A two-piece is slightly more informal but no less favourable, particularly in the warmer months.

The most popular colours for suits are undoubtedly varying shades of grey or blue – these are complementary to practically all skin tones and work well with a vast array of floral décor and other big-day fashion hues that may be used within the bridesmaids' outfits, for example. I'm also a huge fan of texture and prints, particularly herringbone and houndstooth, and you can't beat a gentleman in tweed for a wedding in the countryside.

If it's timeless glamour you're after then a tuxedo is your best friend. Think the archetypal James Bond – you can't go wrong. Trust me, a black-tie dress code never goes out of fashion.

Accessories are a great way to personalise your look, from shoes to buttonholes, cufflinks and watches. One of my favourite wedding parties of all time used a delicate Liberty print that the bride and groom had fallen in love with on an impromptu shopping trip a few months before they were due to be married to perfectly synchronise their wedding party style. The groomsmen's ties and pocket squares were handmade from the fabric, as were the bridesmaids' bouquet bindings, and the flower girls' dresses. The Order of Service stationery even had fine threads of the print within the folded margins.

### Where to buy

Usually the most low-cost option of securing suits, especially multiples if you plan on an extended wedding party, is to hire them. Most suit hire retailers have a wide variety of styles to choose from, in an extensive range of sizes. Hiring is therefore the most relied upon service for larger groups of groomsmen who are required to wear matching outfits.

Alternatively you could opt for ready-to-wear; some mid-price high street stores offer some

good-quality options which can be tailored to fit. Of course you could always blow the budget and buy yourself the ultimate designer suit. And why not? I've often wondered why a groom wouldn't spend as much on a suit as a bride might choose to spend on a dress, within reason of course. Especially as, unlike most wedding gowns, a beautifully-cut suit can be worn again and again.

On the subject of an exquisite cut, it is this that matters the most. Particular styles, colours and materials are a matter of personal preference, but even the most expensive investment will lose its maximum potential if the jacket is too big or the trousers are dragging underneath your heels.

Opting for a made-to-measure or tailored suit is probably the ultimate extravagance, but is undeniably a virtually risk-free choice. Not to mention the added bonus that you can essentially work together with your tailor to create a one-of-a-kind bespoke design if this is the route you go down.

Keeping within the realms of more reasonable budget expectations, visiting a recommended alterations service with any off-the-peg garments you purchase is a must. My husband's high-end high street suit actually came in under our expected spend, but fitted impeccably after a trip to a local experienced dressmaker. He then used the extra cash to treat himself to a luxury pair of brogues. Or maybe I spent it on make-up and perfume … or was it a new bikini for my honeymoon …? I seem to be experiencing sudden and acute memory loss.

I have thus far focused solely on the assumption that a groom does in fact need to wear a suit. Which, of course, he doesn't. The more relaxed and informal the styling of the day, the greater the scope for alternative outfit choices and mixing and matching garments and accessories together.

A pair of colourful chinos and a linen shirt, for example, are ideal for relaxed back garden wedding attire, as is any combination of trouser and casual open-collared shirt. I'm also fond of a long-line khaki short for a coastal celebration and I truly believe a pair of braces can work with almost any outfit to make it the fun side of smart-casual – don't knock it before you try it. The same can be said of hats – everyone I know loves a man in a trilby. Traditional dress and uniform are also winning options and have the potential to make your day even more unique to you as a couple, should your groom feel that he'd like to express this part of his identity on your wedding day.

The key is to try on a variety of styles and fabrics from a range of retailers. Be open-minded; you may be pleasantly surprised by what you discover to be the best option for you.

# Bridesmaids

**Some of my fondest wedding memories are from the time I spent with my best girls on my wedding day. I loved the sense of excitement and anticipation whilst we were getting ready in the morning, glass of champagne in hand, make-up and shoes strewn across every available surface, the overzealous use of hairspray ... a room full of beautiful chaos if you will.**

I was lucky in that I didn't find choosing my bridesmaids difficult at all; my party of four consisted of my two childhood friends, my sister and my soon-to-be sister-in-law. It's about who you want to stand by your side as you say 'I do' to your forever partner, and who you believe will genuinely *want* to take on that role. It shouldn't be about who you feel obliged to ask due to family politics or a mostly unfounded sense of distant historical loyalty. Those are my thoughts on the matter and I shall not be apologising for them either, so neither should you.

In terms of who should fund what when it comes to sartorial bridesmaid purchases, then I hope I can offer some helpful tips. Of course there are no right or wrong answers, just advice based on personal experience.

If you are essentially asking your friends or siblings to wear something very specific that they may not necessarily wear again, then the general consensus is that the cost should form part of the wedding budget. A reasonable compromise if you are more relaxed with what your bridesmaids will be wearing, such as any style of gown but within a certain colour palette, is to set a budget and allow them to fund any extra for a dress they feel they would gain further wear from. They can then choose whether to incur any additional expense or not.

Choosing *what* your bridesmaids should wear is undeniably often a very complex decision. There can be such a range of shapes, sizes and skin tones to consider, not to mention the fact that everybody's tastes can differ dramatically.

I have only two rules to live by:
**a)** Never ask someone you consider a friend to wear something you wouldn't wear yourself.
**b)** If you have duly abided by a) and your bridesmaid raises genuine concerns about her level of comfort in the dress you have in mind, then an alternative option should be offered. What bride would want anyone they care about to be uncomfortable and thus unhappy on their wedding day?

Slightly awkward aspects aside, there is a whole host of options to ensure your favourite ladies look and feel super-stylish as they accompany you on your very special occasion.

### Matchy matchy

Possibly the most recognised and traditional bridesmaids' outfit choice is to have all of your girls in exactly the same design of dress in the same colour. To express each individual's style, you could consider a variation in hairstyles, jewellery and shoes. My girls were all in matching short ivory chiffon dresses, altered to lengths to

suit their height and comfort. They wore their locks how they pleased and each had a similar bouquet but in varying bright shades from my chosen colour palette.

### Same dress, different hue (and vice versa)

Finding a shade that suits all skin tones can be nigh on impossible, therefore if you find the dress of your dreams but the right colour for everyone proves elusive, you could simply have more than one. Both chic *and* problem solving.

In a similar vein, the same hue but different dress has exactly the same appeal.

### Colour palette co-ordinated

Still very cohesive but with more scope for finding styles to suit everyone. Sticking to a colour palette and offering (within reason) mostly free

rein on the design of dress is probably my most favoured option of all. Admittedly there are some palettes that are easier to get right, and seemingly have more availability than others, and these can change depending on fashions that season. But varying shades of blush pink, grey and nude hues are always a winner; classed as neutrals, they are the perfect backdrop for practically any choice of bouquet too.

All I would recommend is to ask your bridesmaids to send you the details of the colour-palette-inspired dress they have found before they make a purchase. I once witnessed a wedding where one of the eight bridesmaids asked to source a gown in a soft sherbet lemon turned up in a shade of yellow that was distinctly on the spectrum of mustard brown. There was no denying she looked very lovely indeed,

but she stood out like a shining beacon. Which should obviously be the job of the bride, exclusively.

True story.

## Pretty in prints

I love a print, and I don't just mean a cute ditzy floral or a minimal polka dot, I mean anything from a statement multi-coloured watercolour effect to geometric shapes and shiny sequin embellishments. Just because it's your wedding day doesn't necessarily mean you or your best girls have to change your usual wardrobe staples for something subtle or twee. Unless you want to, of course.

And if anyone has the audacity to tell you otherwise, respond with the notion that it's *your* day and sometimes it's simply a case of go bold or go home.

## Dress alternatives

I realise this section is purely focused on your bridesmaids wearing gowns, which of course is not the only option as there are no strictly unbreakable wedding rules that anyone should abide by.

Various combinations of skirts and tops can look charming – and offer even more scope for your bridesmaids to express their personal styles and find garments that suit. I particularly love a maxi-length skirt paired with a sweater or long-sleeved cardigan, for the autumn and winter seasons.

Then there are tailored trousers, shorts, culottes or even a playsuit. Potentially any outfit can work, so do keep an open mind when browsing the shop rails or online offerings.

On the subject of buying, we have a selection of specific bridesmaids suppliers listed in our recommended section on pages 208–213 where you can find quality and universally appealing ready-to-wear or made-to-measure outfit suggestions.

Alternatively, the high street offers a wealth of options with every colour, style, neckline and length you could wish for, to suit all manner of budgets and requirements. As long as you don't leave the bridesmaids' dresses shopping until the very last minute, a day of retail therapy with your best girls is a thoroughly enjoyable and fun experience, even more so if you combine it with afternoon tea, a visit to the beauty counters and a cocktail or two.

Just a suggestion.

Another suggestion would be to invite me along . . .

# THE DRESS

# The Dress

But what to wear?! It's a question I ask myself every time I open the doors to my wardrobe, so I can fully sympathise with the seemingly daunting task of finding your fashion mojo when it comes to the main event. I know that, personally, I was completely overwhelmed by the plethora of bridal gown styles available: how was I ever going to find 'The One'?

The best piece of advice I received was to begin by simply considering what regular 'everyday' dress types and shapes I liked, and what suited me the most. At least then I could start somewhere. I knew I preferred straps, a scoop neckline and a fit-and-flare skirt – these particular design elements worked well for my petite frame, so I kept them in mind whilst perusing the seemingly endless rails of froth and fancy.

There may be certain aspects of your wedding that you have already decided on when it comes to choosing your dress, such as the venue or flowers, for example. These prior decisions may have a direct impact on the kind of dress you envisage yourself wearing, as you want to create a cohesive 'look' and, for you, it may not necessarily be about singular elements, but rather your wedding styling as a whole. A stately home backdrop would undoubtedly suit a gown of equal grandeur, and a just-picked bouquet of wild blooms would be the ultimate accessory to a dress with a bohemian free-spirited vibe.

Of course please do feel free to disregard any prior knowledge you have of what you *thought* you wanted prior to the planning of the big day, and try on as many gowns as you see fit. It's not an opportunity you have every day so make the most of the moment. Not to mention the fact you might be in equal parts surprised and thrilled to discover the dress of your dreams is something utterly perfect yet totally unexpected and a complete juxtaposition to everything else on your big day must-have list.

In preparation for any bridal appointment or wedding fashion related shopping expedition I would recommend nude, well-fitting underwear and only taking one or two loyal friends and/or family members with you. Everyone has their own individual taste, which isn't necessarily similar to yours, and too many opinions often end in unnecessary confusion.

Both my sister and my mum accompanied me to one of the first bridal boutique appointments I booked. I tried on what both my mum and I considered to be a rather elegant full-lace overlay number with a pretty puddle train.

After unsuccessfully trying to suppress her laughter my sister announced that I resembled 'a giant doily'.

What to take from my experience? Don't invite my sister to any of your bridal appointments.

# Where to buy

## From a bridal boutique

All over the country there are hundreds of boutiques that stock a select range of bridal gowns from various designers. It is wise to check which designers, as well as which exact dress styles, are available to try on from the associated collections before your appointment to avoid potential disappointment. Depending on timing and availability, most boutiques can request a sample from a designer they stock even if it's not necessarily part of the boutique's permanent line – it's definitely worth calling ahead to check.

Boutique assistants will be able to advise and discuss various styles and shapes with you, and recommend dresses, based on their knowledge and experience, that they feel might suit your requirements. Please be aware some gowns have limited 'hanger' appeal, yet look spectacular once on – I'd advise throwing caution to the wind and giving a few variations a whirl.

Wedding dress sizing differs considerably between styles, and it is unlikely that a sample is going to fit perfectly, regardless of whether it appears to be labelled with your 'size' or not. Boutique assistants are skilled in the temporary fitting of sample gowns, using a variety of tried and tested methods, so you will at least have a genuine indication of how a particular dress would look once it had been altered to fit your specific measurements.

## Direct from the designer

Every bridal designer inevitably has a certain aesthetic that is unique to their brand. You will more than likely find that there are designers you are particularly drawn to as you begin to research various online resources, social media platforms and glossy magazines. The vast majority of designers will have a flagship store where you can admire and try on every single one of their gowns currently in production. Visiting the designer direct is also an opportunity to request bespoke design changes and/or request combinations of various existing dress styles to create a gown that is unique to you, yet still very much within the recommended aforementioned aesthetic.

For either the designer direct or boutique option you will need to pay a deposit for your chosen gown and wait for it to be made and sent to the boutique; six months is normally the recommended time frame, depending on the dress. However, do ensure you ask in advance as some will offer a speedier rush-through service – please be aware there may be extra costs associated.

After your gown has arrived you will then be required to attend another appointment for a fitting, and potentially further fittings, depending on the alterations required. If you do fall in love with a boutique or designer whose flagship store is a considerable distance away, then remember to consider the travel time involved, especially if it's some distance from your venue, as you will only collect your dress a day or two before your wedding. A boutique or designer may be able to recommend a seamstress at a location more convenient for you.

### Ready-to-wear

Many coveted designer labels create the most beautiful gowns that would be more than suitable for your wedding, and in many cases associated costs can actually be very similar to that of a specific bridal dress. You may also feel that a ready-to-wear design is something you will be able to wear again. And again.

The positive of this option is that you are not required to wait for an appointment; a trip to a department store, or a few quick clicks to add a fabulous frock to your virtual basket from any one of the online luxury shopping meccas, means you could be in possession of your gown within 24 hours. It also means if you change your mind, in most instances you have at least a few weeks to send your dress back for a full refund. And then order another one. Or two.

### The high street

Who said you *had* to buy designer anyway? One of the most beautiful brides I have ever seen wore a dress that cost her less than a few hundred pounds from a popular high street chain. The general perception seems to be that in order to feel *special* enough a wedding dress should be a) somewhat expensive and b) unequivocally *bridal*. Neither assumption is true. The dress you choose for your wedding has to be a) a gown you love wearing because it makes you feel confident and beautiful, and b) a gown you love wearing because it makes you feel confident and beautiful.

### Pre-owned/once worn

If you are lucky enough to find 'The One', only to discover it is price-prohibitive, there is always the option of locating the same gown that has been previously owned, often reducing the cost. You can find pre-loved gowns from a variety of websites, sample sales in bridal boutiques, and dedicated charity shops. Please be aware of potential counterfeit goods and make sure you see the dress for yourself and try it on before parting with any cash, as this option is mostly non-refundable.

### Bespoke

You may have a very clear vision of what you want your wedding dress to look like, right down to the lace trim on your capped sleeves. If this is the case then there is an abundance of talented and experienced dressmakers specialising in bridal wear who can directly assist in creating a one-of-a-kind garment that is both made-to-measure and undeniably *you*.

### Vintage/era specific

As per pre-owned, if you are not the slightest bit bothered about wearing 'new', and especially if the idea of a gown with an interesting history makes your heart sing, then you may want to consider a genuine vintage piece. Scouring various specialist vintage markets and shops can be a lot of fun, but potentially time-consuming. There are bridal boutiques who source vintage wedding attire specifically, thus presenting you with what might be a fairytale 1920s flapper dress that you immediately fall head-over-heels in love with. Maximum results, minimum effort.

# Shapes and Styles

There are literally tens of thousands of potential dress designs if you were to endeavour to include every conceivable combination of neckline, fabric, shape, hem length and sleeve style available. You would need a coffee table encyclopaedia just to scratch the surface. And I'm quite sure that at the end of trying to absorb the many, many options available to you, you would be more confused than you were before you started.

I promise I'm not being lazy when I tell you we are not going to attempt anything like an all-singing, all-dancing reference to gowns you could *potentially* wear. Instead, we're sharing some of the most popular shapes paired with an assortment of additional design elements that might take your fancy. Or, at least, this section might emphasise which dresses you *don't* love; sometimes it's the ruthless elimination process that highlights the styles that will unfold as most suited to you.

**1 Shape: Ballgown**
*'Nicoletta'* **by Hayley Paige**
Nicoletta is an ethereal ballgown silhouette, consisting of a full-tiered tulle skirt and a ballet-inspired sequin bodice with delicate criss-cross back detail in Alabaster.

**2 Shape: Sheath**
*'Style 714'* **by Martina Liana**
Featuring a silk Moroccan skirt with a Parisian silk chiffon bodice, which drapes over a belt detail of encrusted Swarovski crystals.

**3 Shape: Midi Length/Separates**
*'Dee'* **Skirt,** *'Darla'* **Bodice and** *'Dahlia'* **Lace Topper by Catherine Deane**
The Catherine Deane draped silk tulle Dee skirt combined with the Darla duchess satin bodice and Dahlia high-collar lace topper work together to create a a bridal ensemble that is as effortless as it is chic. The scalloped lace overlay can be removed for an alternative look that is both contemporary and perfect for warm summer evenings.

**4 Shape: Fishtail**
*'Celia'* Corset by Martina Liana
& *'Amina'* Skirt by Watters
Celia is a shape-enhancing, zip-back corset featuring lace appliqué and a sweetheart neckline. The Amina skirt is constructed from draped ivory tulle featuring a dramatic flare at the knees.

**5 Shape: Slimline**
*'Eloise'* by Anna Campbell
Constructed from silk and topped with delicate lace, the Eloise has a clean, slimline silhouette complete with a lace and sequin train.

**6 Shape: A-Line**
*'Esme'* by Kate Halfpenny
Esme is a strapless soft corseted dress with a full circle skirt. The fabric is a delicious embroidered organza that makes a perfect A-line silhouette.

# Coloured Wedding Dresses

The vast majority of wedding gowns are white or on the spectrum of white, from the brightest dazzling true white to delicate ivory to a rich golden buttercream and of course everything in between. Even though these hues may appear to be very similar, they can actually look incredibly different once on, depending on your skin tone. Not to mention the fact that one designer's 'champagne' could be another's 'eggshell'.

As it turns out, not all lighter shades of pale are created equal.

If you find the dress of your dreams yet you are simply unsure about the colour, the style may be available in a myriad of alternatives, so it definitely pays to ask your supplier the question. Once you are confident in your shade selection, it is worth requesting a fabric swatch, so that you are able to compare and contrast with your accessories, shoes and other fashion considerations within your wedding party, such as bridesmaid and flower girl outfit choices.

Of course there are absolutely no hard-and-fast rules indicating you are required to have a 'white wedding' at all, and there is an increasing selection of gowns available in light feminine tones within the majority of boutiques. Soft shades of blush, grey and blue in particular are popular, as well as overtly embellished bridal wear that has the overall effect of shimmering your way down the aisle in glistening golds, silvers and pewter hues.

You may wish to move away from a muted colour palette altogether; my mum chose to say 'I do' in royal blue, the prettiest crêpe two-piece suit complete with swishy skirt, floral hat and nude wedge sandals. She looked amazing, and very much the bride, regardless of her decision not to wear what would be considered a more traditional ensemble.

And talking of ensembles, who said you had to wear a *dress* anyway? A tailored jacket and trousers à la Bianca Jagger, or in fact any combination of separates, can be equally elegant, not to mention perhaps more suited to your usual tastes and existing everyday wardrobe choices.

Anything goes. Any style, any colour. It's about feeling confident and comfortable and, most importantly, it's about feeling the best and most beautiful version of *you*.

# Questions to ask your Boutique

### How should I prepare for my initial bridal appointment?

- Ring ahead to ensure the bridal retailer you wish to visit has the exact dress design samples in stock that you want to try on; boutiques often only carry a small selection of a designer's range.

- You may want to check whether the boutique offers individual appointments or whether there will be other brides there at the same time. You may not mind either way but the experience undoubtedly differs.

- Wear underwear that fits well and will work with a number of gown styles and fabrics; a nude multi-way bra and no-VPL matching knickers is a favourable option.

### How long will my bridal gown take to come into stock?

- Most bridal retailers recommend ordering your gown six months in advance of your wedding date to ensure there is enough time for fittings and alterations. There are sometimes speedier services available but there may be extra cost implications.

### How much will my alterations cost?

- After you have chosen your dress, your retailer should be able to give you an indication of the expected basic alteration costs. Of course, if you have requested bespoke design alterations rather than just altered-to-fit changes, costs can increase considerably.

- **Made-to-order** is when your dress is ordered from a standard size chart and cut from an existing pattern as close to your individual measurements as possible (usually bust, waist and hip measurements). There is every chance that you will require alterations to ensure a perfect fit.

- **Made-to-measure** means your dress is made specifically for you, to your exact measurements, of which around 25 are taken. A 'toile' is created, which is a cotton mock-up of the bodice of your wedding dress that is fitted exactly to your body in order to replicate what your dress will look like when complete. This can then be tweaked as needed before your real wedding dress is constructed. Understandably, made-to-measure dresses often command a much higher investment.

### How many fittings will I require?

- On average you will need at least two fittings. The first will be when your gown comes into stock at your boutique, and will be to take exact measurements for any potential alterations, and the second will be nearer to the wedding date to ensure the perfect fit.

- Made-to-measure options may only require one fitting, should your measurements remain the same as they were on the date of the initial order.

200
SPANISH
LACE PINS
CORRESPONDANCE
MERCHANT & MILLS
DRAPER
BODKIN & THREADER

CHAPTER FIVE

# ACCESSORIES

# Accessories

Adding the finishing touches to my bridal ensemble was the aspect of the planning process I was looking forward to the most. A self-confessed magpie to the core, I am a purveyor of the shiny and the statement, so shopping for my accessories should have been a thoroughly enjoyable and relatively straightforward experience.

Famous last words. I look back and eye roll at my own naivety.

Accessorising was the one area where I completely lost my sense of personal style. I took one look at my go-to collection of chunky rings, multiple jangly bracelets and overtly embellished cuffs and decided they simply were not *bridal* enough. And that I required jewellery that was dainty and delicate and therefore the epitome of elegance.

After a time-consuming and unsuccessful search for what I perceived to be exactly the right pieces for my wedding day, I opted for bespoke, and designed a co-ordinating set of clear crystal drop bead earrings and a matching necklace. The more I worried about creating something timeless, the more delicate and dainty my design ideas became. To the point where, when the items finally arrived, although admittedly very pretty, you could hardly notice they were well ... *there*.

So imperceptible was my choice of big day ornamentation that in my wedding photographs you can't actually tell I am wearing any jewellery at all. No evidence of the shiny and the statement, not a sign of the familiar magpie *me*.

Then there's the question of footwear. I am not actually that *into* shoes as it happens (I can imagine many of you audibly gasp at this unexpected admission, but it's true). I like ankle boots. Or ... ankle boots. When I discovered a pair of designer gunmetal-grey peep-toe sandals at half price I snapped them up immediately; they might not have been a cute boot but they were so luxe! And such a bargain! And unexpectedly clashed with the particular ivory shade of my gown.

I only realised this fact a week before the date of our nuptials when I actually remembered to try my shoes on with my wedding dress. Cue a frantic case of last-minute online ordering of various styles, hues and heel heights in the vain hope that *something* would work.

I settled on a pair of very plain pointy-toe mules, which were comfortable enough, but certainly not the kind of design I would ever normally try on, let alone consider wearing for such a special occasion.

Last but not least I went through what is now fondly remembered as 'veil gate'. I was certain from the off that I wasn't going to wear one. That was until my sister, mum and seemingly the majority of my female friends were really quite adamant that a veil was the *ultimate* accessory when completing your transformation into the quintessential 'bride'. I did a whole one-eighty and went from no veil to full cathedral length, complete with subtle yet twinkly sequin detail and the firm belief that it was the right and proper decision. Besides, I had to make up for my almost invisible jewellery.

When it came to the day itself, the veil did not sit in my hair-do particularly well, no matter how many times the comb attachment was re-arranged. My dad then proceeded to trample on the hem of the damn thing the entire way up the aisle. Honestly, the photographic evidence is hilarious.

I should have worn statement jewellery that was 'me', I should have worn a pair of the most spectacular ankle boots, and I should have stuck to my guns and not bothered with the veil at all. Or at least endeavoured to ensure my dad wasn't a right clumsy so-and-so.

Should've, would've, could've. Whatever. In the grand scheme of things my accessory-related woes did not at all hinder the wonderful wedding day I had. But my personal experience does mean I can confidently advise on how *you* might avoid making similar blunders with your choice of bridal adornments.

## Jewellery

I love it when a bride chooses to wear just one item of look-at-me jewellery, be it a full-on diamante choker or shoulder-sweeping chandelier earrings. Equally there is something very personal and timeless about wearing pieces for the big day that you wear *every* day, and that carry with them some kind of sentiment or precious memory.

I often hear of brides being gifted jewellery by their parents or grandparents in the lead-up to the wedding that has been in the family for generations. It's incredibly special to wear something that brings with it so much history.

However, if you are quite positive you are not in the running for an heirloom any time soon (me neither, unfortunately) you could consider purchasing some new fine jewellery – investing in a truly beautiful piece that not only will you wear for decades to come, but you can pass on to future family members. I'm not suggesting everyone should blow the budget on a diamond pendant but, you know, price per wear and all that.

Unless you had your heart set on something in particular immediately following your engagement, it might be wise to purchase your jewels after you have found your gown. With necklaces in particular, it is important to consider the neckline design of your dress as it will determine the length of necklace you opt for. You certainly don't want your carefully selected necklace to be hidden, or continually catching the top of your bodice.

On the subject of catching, please be mindful of the fastening detail of bracelets, as I have heard of many a disappointed bride who has suffered continual damage to the fine lace or silk chiffon of her gown from pointy closure mechanisms. Tears in your fancy frock for the sake of accessories, no matter how covetable the pieces might appear initially, are undisputedly *not* chic.

As well as decorating your earlobes, wrists and neckline you may also be contemplating a specific flourish for your head and/or hair. It's often as much the way you wear your chosen headpiece as the design itself that determines the perceived style. A decorative band worn

across your forehead is decidedly more bohemian in vibe than if you were to wear it across your crown, for example. That's not to say you can't or shouldn't mix up styles to create your very own unique look. In fact I actively encourage it. One of the most memorable show-stopping brides I have ever seen chose to wear classic simple pearl studs combined with her grandmother's costume statement sapphire necklace and a full-on faux flower crown. Not like anything I had seen before or since, but very, *very* much 'her'.

If you do have your heart set on wearing a headpiece, please do make sure you try it on with your chosen hairstyle before the big day, not only to confirm they work well combined, but to ensure a secure fit.

No bride wants a tiara falling into her crème brûlée during the speeches.

## Shoes

If you have chosen a floor-length gown then the likelihood is that your shoes will not be on show for the vast majority of the day. You will also be wearing your shoes for an *entire* day. Or at least from the ceremony to the reception in the evening, and therefore at least some level of comfort is key.

That's not to say your wedding shouldn't be the perfect excuse to own the sky-high stilettos of your dreams, but if you can only bear standing in them for ten minutes, you should probably consider an equally aesthetically pleasing, yet more wearable, alternative.

Of course there is always the option to buy an exquisite pair for your aisle debut and various photo opportunities, and then another perhaps more *sensible* option for late night drinking and dance floor frolics.

Yes, I am advising you that purchasing two pairs of shoes for your wedding is perfectly acceptable.

Unlike yours truly (see earlier for my own disaster story), please, *please* try to decide on your footwear with plenty of time before your wedding so that the hemline of your gown can be altered accordingly and that you are 100 per cent happy that the colour combination and overall look is what you had in mind. Sometimes what we imagine in our head is considerably different to the reality of the mirror reflection.

## Cover-ups

Even if you are lucky enough to experience a warm summer's day as you say 'I do', when the sun sets it can in some places often become distinctly chillier. And for autumn and winter brides especially, the idea of exposing bare arms to the seasonal elements probably isn't that appealing.

I think an additional cover-up accessory for the evening is as practical as it is pretty, and a great way to give your bridal ensemble an alternative look for the twilight hours.

A fine-knit cardigan in your favourite colour will look cosy and elegant, as will a faux fur stole or a cashmere pashmina, or indeed any combination of the aforementioned fabrics and styles.

Don't feel you have to invest in a new cover-up for your wedding just because you feel you need a garment that is perceived as traditionally bridal – your everyday leather jacket or long tweed coat are effortlessly edgy when combined with a sumptuous gown.

Of course you may not be concerned about outwitting the cold, but simply want to add a little extra glamour to your outfit over all. In that case a delicate sequin, embellished or beaded shrug gets my vote.

## Veils

To veil or not to veil? That is the question. And to assist with what still might be a 'not sure', we've put together the ultimate guide.

The way your veil moves and falls is not only dependent on the quantity of material but also the edging detail. A full lace edge is where the lace runs all the way around the veil, right up to the comb attachment. A semi (or demi) lace edge will end around shoulder height, and cut edge veils have no edging at all; they are the lightest in weight and thus have the most movement.

You can also choose from a single-tier or a two-tier veil. A two-tier has an additional layer of fabric often referred to as a 'blusher' that goes over the bride's face. The blusher is often raised during the first kiss or at the exact moment you are pronounced married. Once raised it is swept back over the head to form a second layer at the back of the veil.

As there is such a variety of designs, length and trim details to choose from, you are sure to find the style that's perfect for you.

## The Veil Guide

The most popular style of veil is known as the 'classic', which is traditionally created from tulle.

A classic veil is available in various different lengths:

**Cathedral length:** 300cm long, the most dramatic in terms of train.

**Church and/or chapel length:** 250cm.

**Floor length:** These are 200cm long, or slightly shorter, depending on your height.

**Ballet length:** 150cm in length and falling around the mid-calf.

**Fingertip:** 122cm in length and falling below your elbow and fingertips, again depending on your height.

Of course you may want something a little different to the classic styles, in which case you could consider the following:

**Bandeau veil:** This is a very small veil that is attached to either side of the head and is often made from net.

**Drop veil:** A simple style that is often held in place with a headband, this falls over the face and down the back. The Duchess of Cambridge wore a drop veil on her wedding day.

**Birdcage veil:** Similar to bandeau in style but these are attached to the top of the crown and typically cover the top portion of the face. They originally became popular in the 1940s.

**Juliette veil:** Often referred to as a 'Juliette cap' after the cap of fabric that holds the veil in place, these veils originate from the sixteenth century and were very popular with brides in the 1920s and 1930s.

As with all other accessories, please do try on your veil with your gown, allowing enough time before your wedding date to make changes should they be required. You should check colour, fit and the way the veil drapes and falls with the fabric of your dress. I would also recommend walking with your veil on in front of a mirror so you can gain a clear idea of movement.

Something old, something new, something borrowed and something blue – those final touches can really add the wow factor and personalise your look. However, if all you really want to wear in terms of accessories is your engagement ring and wedding band then that's perfectly ok too. There is undeniable elegance in the art of simplicity.

# Underwear

**We need to talk about lingerie. Particularly knickers and bras. Specifically knickers and bras that fit to absolute perfection with no risk of being seen, until the time comes that you want to show them off.**

I can't begin to express how important it is to ensure your underwear is virtually imperceptible on your wedding day. It needs to feel comfortable, supportive and form a smooth foundation for whatever gorgeous ensemble you have chosen to wear as you walk down the aisle. Trust me when I tell you that one of the major regrets I've heard from umpteen brides is that their underpinnings simply didn't do the job they were supposed to. Not to mention the fact I very nearly had an incredibly embarrassing incident on the dance floor on my big day because my bra cups decided they would like to take residence under my chin whilst I was indulging in some rather exuberant twirling action. The less said about that the better.

Of course there are dresses that don't require a bra – those that are designed to be worn without or that have built-in corsetry that acts as support for your bust. In that case, it's simply the pursuit of a pretty pair of pants.

Traditional lace bridal lingerie is feminine and elegant, but is easily detected through fine silk or figure-hugging chiffon. And a pair of stockings may indeed be ever so sexy, but perhaps not so much when you can see the outline of a suspender belt underneath your delicate satin sheath.

What I am endeavouring to say is, unless you are wearing a very underwear-forgiving ballgown style of dress with multi layers of fabric and straps wide enough to cover those of your bra, I would highly recommend the following:

**1** Have a bra fitting with a specialist, even if you have been measured fairly recently – your size can change.

**2** Try on different brands of bra in your size until you find one that is super secure yet also supremely comfortable. This may take some time, I know, but I promise it will be worth it.

**3** Take the bra you wish to wear on your wedding day to your first dress fitting, not only to make sure there are no unwanted surprises in terms of it not quite creating the shape you expected, but also so your gown can be fitted to take into account the design and/or the extra enhancement padding your bra may include.

**4** Try on your chosen knickers with your dress prior to the day, just to make sure there are no visible seams that show through the material of your gown. The same goes for stockings or hold-ups.

If you are looking for shape wear, then there is a wide variety of flattering one pieces available from most department stores to choose from. I often find that brides shy away from considering,

say, a pair of knicker shorts with high-waisted built-in tummy control, because they fear it may not be the most desirable style of lingerie to expose on their wedding night. In that case treat yourself to a separate set of smalls to change into after your guests have left and you have retired to the bedroom, because who said you couldn't?

And finally, we also need to talk about garters. I think they are darling – and they are having a bit of a revival right now. Think velvet ribbon with French lace and seed pearl detailing, the more luxurious the better.

A garter need no longer be associated with cheap thrills; it's all about seeking out the most decadent *frills*.

# CHAPTER SIX

# FINISHING TOUCHES

# Hair

I am officially terrible at doing anything remotely glamorous or sophisticated with my own hair. I can manage 'bedhead' quite easily, i.e. get out of bed, backcomb the roots a bit and don't bother to brush the rest of it. Sometimes I'll maybe spray in some dry shampoo so I don't resemble the great unwashed, but that's about the extent of my styling skills.

It was paramount therefore for my own wedding that I employed the services of a professional hair stylist; someone who could recreate the look that was in my head, but wouldn't (like me) burn themselves repeatedly with the curling wand. (Every. Time.)

I wear my long hair down the vast majority of the time; it's how my husband prefers it, and it's how I feel most like 'me', so I was never going to opt for something drastically different for the big day. That's not to say you shouldn't experiment with different styles, you just need to make absolutely sure that a) you love the way it looks and b) you will feel comfortable for a whole day and evening with your chosen do.

There are obviously styles that fare better in wet or humid conditions, namely those that are swept away from the face and neck and pinned fairly substantially, thus preventing pesky flyaways and frizz. However, the right products and techniques should mean that whatever look you choose, your locks should always appear luscious.

I would definitely consider the design of your gown before finalising any hairstyle choices, particularly for dresses that have an embellished or statement back design; it would seem a shame to cover the majority with thick waves, for example, no matter how glossy.

With regard to the many different styles you could choose for your wedding day, only you know your hair type, how it behaves and how you like to wear it. Please don't assume you must choose from a list of traditionally *bridal* hairstyles either. Anything is possible.

A ballerina bun is universally flattering, as is a French plait or a braided crown, and I've yet to see anyone who doesn't suit a bouncy cheerleader-style ponytail. All of which can be updated dramatically with the addition of a judiciously chosen accessory or a selection of flowers.

Please do ensure you try your preferred hair accessory with your chosen hairstyle during a trial, and ask your hair stylist – or a bridesmaid if you are styling your hair yourself – to check, and double check, that your headpiece, be it a glitzy headband or a single bloom, is pinned in as securely as possible.

If longevity is your main concern, then from my experience of styling models on numerous photoshoots, attending many weddings with perfectly coiffed brides and featuring thousands more on the blog, the aforementioned plait just might be your best friend. Even if you plan on wearing your hair loose, a few tiny braids amongst curls or waves add texture and can prevent layers

from becoming limp and lacklustre. I'm also a fan of the hair 'roll', which sits at the nape of the neck. It is extremely elegant and holds well throughout the day, whilst still looking soft and feminine. A roll looks particularly pretty when adorned with small flower heads or subtly shimmering hairpins.

Call me old-fashioned (or perhaps retro even) but nothing says chic like a chignon. An excellent choice of up-do should you want to go all Miss Moneypenny and quickly change your look to swinging-around-your-shoulders for the evening reception. A chignon works just as well for shorter hair as it does for long.

On the subject of shorter hair, please don't feel the need to go to extreme lengths (!) just because it's your wedding day. If a pixie crop is your signature style then wear it down the aisle with pride.

And I know I mentioned bedhead earlier as if it was a bad thing, but believe me it's not. Deliberately messy hair is possibly my favourite style of all: undeniably sexy and with the added bonus of being incredibly low maintenance.

Consider the design of your gown before finalising any hairstyle choices, particularly for dresses that have an embellished or statement back design.

# Make-up

Unless you are a model or serial selfie taker, your wedding day is the one occasion in your life where you will be constantly photographed. I know from personal experience, and from the thousands of brides we have featured on rockmywedding.co.uk, that this can be an extraordinarily daunting prospect.

Most of us have a set beauty routine of sorts – a trusted skincare regime followed by various cosmetics that enhance our favourite features. Firstly I'd just like to muscle in here with the bold statement that you don't have to change the way you look just because you're getting married. Your partner is making a lifelong commitment to you because well, you are you. Occasional unruly brows and all.

That's not to say that we shouldn't want to look the very best version of ourselves on our wedding day; of course we should. Especially when – like it or not – as the bride you are going to be the pinnacle of popularity 24/7.

My first piece of advice would be to ask yourself how confident you are at applying your own make-up. If you are comfortable doing it yourself, and wince at the thought of someone else waving a mascara wand really, *really* close to your eyeball, then attempting to paint your own face is probably the right choice for you. However, a trip to one (or several) of your favourite beauty counters will be beneficial – some are more specialist than others with regard to bridal consultations. I would suggest calling ahead to enquire about expertise and availability, and to book an allocated appointment; if there is a chargeable fee this is more often than not redeemable against purchase. With just a few helpful hints from the experts, you can pick up some valuable tips and tricks and sample products that you may not have otherwise considered, and that could transform your normal, routine quick-and-easy into something a little more special.

I find the most frequent concern raised is about the staying power of make-up for the day itself – I'm sure no one wants to spend any longer than necessary powdering their nose when they could be sipping cocktails and dancing with friends. Apologies in advance if I am preaching to the converted but there is a primer for EVERYTHING. A primer to smooth away pores and fine lines and significantly increase the wear of your foundation, a primer to ensure eyeliner and shadow adheres and doesn't fade or crease, even specific pout primers that prevent lipstick bleed and feathering. Definitely worth the investment if you feel that by lunchtime your morning-applied perfectly-executed-brisk-walk blush has left the building.

I would also recommend a water-resistant mascara in case of tears (of pure unadulterated joy *obviously*) and if the thought of any potential black smudges underneath your lower lids fills you with dread, semi-permanent eyelash extensions or daily glue-on falsies are a viable option.

If you are less than confident with your application technique or would just rather relax on the morning of your wedding day with the aforementioned cocktail, there are many experienced and talented make-up artists who will ensure those unruly brows are groomed and that shiny T-zone is a distant memory.

If you do decide to go down the professional supplier route please have a trial, or two if you are not 100 per cent pleased with the first attempt. Trials are chargeable and most make-up artists charge per member of the wedding party rather than a flat rate or hourly rate. Some make-up artists will also bring an assistant along if there are lots of people to get through, which will also incur extra costs. If there are particular products, textures and colours that you love, and make you feel confident, then your make-up artist should be only too willing to incorporate your requests into the finished look, or at least suggest alternatives of an equal quality and finish.

With any new product purchase or beauty treatment please, please ensure you trial them at least three months before the big day, in case of a potentially adverse reaction.

This is the part where I emphasise yet again that, just because you are the bride, you really, *really* shouldn't feel you have to change your look for something that is traditionally 'bridal'. The description 'natural' is often promoted when it comes to the perceived perfect wedding day make-up, ironically often requiring you to use umpteen products in order to look as though you are hardly wearing anything at all. Wear as much or as little as makes you feel happy, confident and camera-ready.

If an edgy feline liner flick is your signature style, then do it; the same goes for a smoky eye or a bold lip. And of course if you don't really wear make-up full stop then it's not necessary to do so for this one particular occasion.

Some of you may do nothing more than smudge a kohl pencil around your peepers, and prefer the way it looks the following day after you've slept in it. Which is also absolutely fine.

Hot mess is also good. *Really* good.

# Nails

For some, beautifying fingertips is very low on the priority list when it comes to their big day. With so many other preparations to consider, I'm not in the least bit surprised. And for others, the perfect manicure is an integral part of the package. Either way, it is worth considering how you'd like your nails to look on your wedding day.

It may or may not come as a surprise that your hands are often a focus point of attention throughout your wedding day, as much as any other personal detail. Your friends and family will undoubtedly want to admire your new shiny wedding band, and that bouquet isn't going to carry itself. (Admittedly, you may enlist one of your bridesmaids to be the beholder of blooms and in that case she needs to maintain neat cuticles too, ok?)

I am officially useless at my own manicure. I have invested in a plethora of implements and treatments that have promised to produce talons of impenetrable steel, only for my nails to peel and break as per usual. And don't get me started on attempting to paint them: I never fail to smudge, chip and ruin my work within 24 hours, no matter which fancy quick-dry topcoat I diligently apply.

If you are supremely skilled in producing an even, glossy glow that seems to last forever, I am green-eyed with jealousy. Creating the perfect bridal manicure yourself is probably a walk in the park.

For the rest of us, I would heartily recommend a trip to a professional manicurist, who will ensure your nails are buffed and beautiful for all of those extreme close-ups. If you really want to guarantee a long-lasting finish you could consider a gel overlay, which – from (extensive) experience – is basically foolproof. Essentially you have very fine coats of gel applied to your nail beds, which are then 'cured' (in other words, set) by a UV lamp. The finish is very similar to regular nail polish.

I opted for a set of gel overlays for my wedding, and my manicure lasted until long after I had returned from honeymoon, even after extensive exposure to chlorine and copious applications of

sun cream. As a result of this undeniable longevity I now have a very expensive addiction.

In terms of what colour you should choose, well, that really *is* the fun part. There is no denying that a simple French polish is timeless and elegant, and if it's what you feel comfortable with then go ahead, you can absolutely guarantee that it will work with all colour schemes, gown fabrics and accessories. Similarly, other neutrals such as beiges, delicate nudes or pale pinks can't fail to provide a complementary backdrop to your gorgeous rings.

Strong, bold shades can also look amazing, especially when you have otherwise kept to a fashion palette of traditional bridal ivory hues. I've witnessed equally covetable cobalt blue, burgundy and matt grey manicures as well as summery corals, pretty peaches and classic red. Anything goes.

Of course, you may also want to incorporate nail art and create your own unique design. And why not? Like I said, your nails are such a focal point.

As with any new product or beauty treatment please do make sure you test appropriately, well in advance of your wedding day, for any potential adverse reactions.

# Perfume

'That smells like heaven …' was my now husband's reaction upon perusing the shiny fragrance counter of a fancy department store and discovering what was to become my 'wedding' perfume.

Who knew there was such a thing? Not I, that's for sure. A friend advised me that apparently every bride should endeavour to find a fragrance specifically for the big day, and that this mission was as important as deciding upon all of your other accessories and final flourishes. Of course this was said with a generous pinch of tongue-in-cheek, and you may already wear a signature scent that you are more than happy to waft on your wrist as you say 'I do'.

As it happens, my wedding day perfume became one of my favourite finishing touches. I continued to wear it throughout our honeymoon and, even now, several years later, a quick spritz doesn't fail to evoke memories of such a joyous occasion.

A little part of me is indeed simply enabling you to purchase a new pretty bottle to decorate your dressing table and look uber lovely in photographs, but that's ok. If you can't treat yourself on what is to be one of the most memorable days of your life then when can you?

## If you can't treat yourself on what is to be one of the most memorable days of your life then when can you?

CHAPTER SEVEN.

# FLOWERS

You can also add volume and height to any arrangements by using lush greenery and foliage, often significantly more cost-effective per stem than flowers themselves.

If you or your loved ones happen to be expertly green-fingered, then you may be more than confident in purchasing flowers wholesale and creating your own floral arrangements, in which case I salute you. I now know my lilacs from my lisianthus, due to my career choices, but it takes fortitude and conviction to spend the evening before, or the morning of your big day, potentially trimming thorny stalks whilst your hands are frequently submerged in cold water. Call me a wimp, or just plain lazy, but I would rather remove any potential risk element and leave as much as I can to the professionals.

A skilled and experienced florist will be able to assist in making sure you are able to maximise your budget and offer truly special floral details to complement the style of your day.

**We have included advice on how to choose the right florist for you, with important questions you should ask them, on page 136.**

# The Bouquet

**As your bouquet is essentially the piece of floral décor that is likely to be photographed the most, and certainly a key part of your personal bridal look, it's a logical place to begin when considering what flowers you would like to incorporate into your wedding day as a whole.**

There is a wide variety of bouquet styles to choose from, the most popular falling into the following categories: neat, compact and symmetrical; 'hand-picked' and rustic; statement and trailing; or 'organic', with little to no defined structure. We have included examples of these styles using blooms that are specific, and thus readily available, for every season on pages 120–127. This is by no means a definitive selection, but a helpful guide and starting point. You can easily create a truly one-of-a-kind design by mixing and matching different hues, textures and various varieties of flowers and foliage.

When it comes to bouquets for bridesmaids and keeping your florals cohesive, a smaller version of your own bouquet is a frequently favoured choice. I personally adore the idea of each bridesmaid having a different bouquet but still keeping within the colour scheme, or at least including one of the flower varieties from the bridal bouquet in their own arrangement. From a cost perspective, a delicate wrist corsage or a pomander use fewer blooms so are often considerably cheaper, whilst equally charming.

As well as the arrangement and selection of flowers you choose, there are many additional decorative ways in which you can personalise your bouquet; pretty ribbons, printed fabrics and colourful yarns can be used around the stems of your florals to add interest and potentially tie into other areas of wedding décor.

A popular and meaningful way to accessorise your bouquet is to add a locket containing the photographs of those whose memory you wish to celebrate on your special day, such as a grandparent or other close relative who can't be with you. We also love the addition of trailing strings of sequins for those of you who wish to incorporate a smidgen of shimmer and subtle glamour.

In terms of caring for your bouquet throughout the day, there will be times when you are not holding it, so it's always wise to have a vessel of water to hand for you to use. Some blooms are very hardy whereas others are distinctly more perishable, particularly in warmer climates. A friend of mine placed pretty vases on a centrally positioned table in the post-ceremony drinks area for her and her bridesmaids' bouquets. Not only did this make for a beautiful décor display but it also meant she and her best girls were able to mingle hands-free.

It has long been a tradition for the bride to 'throw' her bouquet, with the intention of being caught by a guest who will allegedly gain good fortune and potentially be next in line to marry.

I'm not particularly superstitious but there is no denying this ritual makes for much hilarity and amusing photo opportunities. I know many brides who have flatly refused to part with their bouquet all day, because they love it so much, let alone potentially gift it to someone else. They have often then gone on to have their bouquet preserved as a lovely memento of the day. Some florists will also offer to make a secondary, smaller version of your bouquet, specifically for the intention of tossing it, but do be aware that this will normally incur extra costs.

I had every intention of tossing my giant pouf of hydrangea, but it slipped my mind in the midst of all the fun and frolics. In hindsight my bouquet was so heavy this was possibly a fortuitous case of forgetfulness; I'm unsure as to the potential safety hazard of such a large and weighty object flying through the air, especially when the thrower has decidedly questionable aim.

# Spring Bouquets

'Spring flowers can leak sap, so make sure you take
them out of water about half an hour before you
leave for the wedding, to give the stems a chance
to seal over and dry before going anywhere near your
dress – the perfect job for one of your bridesmaids!'

Advice and flowers by Emily Wisher
emilywisherartisanflorist.co.uk

Clematis Pirouette, Thalia Narcissi, bluebells,
grape hyacinths and sweet peas

Ranunculus, David Austin roses, lilac, Viburnum,
sweet peas, hyacinths, Parrot tulips and Eucalyptus

Various double daffodils and Golden Trumpets, tulips, *Pieris japonica* and Narcissi

Hellebores, nigella, camellia with its greenery, *Viburnum opulus*, fern, trailing Jasmine and Eucalyptus

Parrot tulips, Lisianthus, Ranunculus, sweet peas and Narcissi

Ranunculus, sweet peas, dogwood foliage, asparagus fern and camellia foliage

# Summer Bouquets

'If you want to bring the outside in then ask your florist to check what flowers are planted in the grounds of your venue and include these in your seasonal flower choices for your bouquet and table centres.'

Advice and flowers by Karen Morgan
passionforflowers.net

Lilac

Soft pink Astilbe

Coral Charm peony, peach Lisianthus, soft pink Astilbe, 'Miss Piggy' rose, 'Juliet' David Austin rose, Jasmine

White peony, white stock, white lilac, nigella, white Astilbe, Thalespi, fountain grass, Amni, Gypsophila, *Viburnum opulus* 'Roseum'

Purple and lilac sweet peas

'Juliet' David Austin rose, 'Keira' David Austin rose, 'Patience' David Austin rose, Tanacetum, Amni, Thalespi, Lisianthus

# Autumn Bouquets

'To keep your bouquet looking fresh after the big day itself, simply cut the stems at an angle and place in clean water. If you can keep your bouquet in a cool environment and replace the water every couple days then you'll be enjoying your blooms for days after the wedding.'

Advice and flowers by Jemma Gade
thecountryflowercompany.com

Ranunculus, Avalanche roses, Brunia, Astrantia, *Eucalyptus populus*, Dusty Miller, Snowberries

Acapella roses, Ranunculus, Chocolate cosmos, Viburnum berrries, Astrantia, Earl Grey roses, Sedum, *Eucalyptus parvi*, Pheasant feathers

Ranunculus, Clematis, Blanchette spray roses, 'Juliet' David Austin roses, Sedum, Astranita, Olive, Bacarra roses, Pittosporum

Acapella roses, Menta roses, Snowberries, Astrantia, Dusty Miller, *Eucalyptus populus*

Ranunculus, Chocolate cosmos, 'Juliet' David Austin roses, Talea roses, *Eucalyptus populus ruud*, First Lady roses

Hydrangea, Pink Faith roses, Amnesia roses, Earl Grey roses, Quicksand roses, Blanchette spray roses, Ranunculus, Viburnum berries, Clematis, Cymbidium orchid, Dusty Miller, *Eucalyptus populus*, Leatherleaf, Royal Purple leaf

# Winter Bouquets

'Flowers may be more limited in availability and choice in Winter but this means that creativity is required in abundance to make each one unique. Take your inspiration from nature and look into using seed heads, berries and foliage in amongst the flowers to create something really stunning.'

Advice and flowers by Sarah Pike
mrs-umbels.co.uk

Ranunculus, Anemones, *Ornithogalum saundersiae*, Matthiola, Veronica, Eustoma, Delphiniums

Ranunculus – white/pink/burgundy, Anemones, 'Keira' David Austin rose

Tulip Ronaldo, Rose Black Baccara, Quicksand rose, *Chrysanthemum Barca*, *Scabiosa stellata*, Viburnum berries, Eucalyptus foliage

Raw cotton, Raw cotton casings/seed pods

Pink Ranunculus, Pink Eustoma, Earl Grey rose, *Chrysanthemum rossano*, *Senecio cineraria*, *Kaaps brunia*

Hyacinths, Hellebores

# Floral Décor

Even the smallest floral flourish can assist in personalising your wedding styling, as well as simply making everything that little bit prettier. You can use flowers to decorate various areas of your venue, or indeed yourself and your wedding party, in any which way you please. In this section we've included some popular and effective ideas that will hopefully prove helpful and inspiring when deciding on your big day floral décor.

### Table centres

Most couples choose to incorporate an arrangement of blooms in the centre of each table for the wedding breakfast (please refer to pages 172–173 for a detailed diagram on potential positioning). If you choose to have round tables, the height and density of the floral styling will have a direct impact on whether your guests are able to view each other across the table or not. The most favoured option therefore is either low – so you are able to see over the top – or very high with a slimline vessel you can see around, in order to increase the socialising and merriment opportunities.

Matching arrangements for each table is a simple and elegant choice, which instantly makes the space appear cohesive. You could also consider having the same choice of blooms but in varying heights and designs so each table is slightly different, or indeed the same variety of flower but a different colour for each table. A combination of florals and candles creates a romantic atmosphere for wedding breakfasts that take place later on in the evening, and the addition of extra non-floral decorative props can create a completely bespoke set-up that is personal to you.

### Garlands

Garlands can be draped across a range of fittings and fixtures, from a stair banister to a doorframe, mantelpiece or windowsill, and are the epitome of luxury and opulence. Often created predominantly from greenery, you can also add any combination of flowers, allowing it to tie in with your bouquet and colour palette.

As garlands are not submerged in water once they have been set up, I would advise discussing with your florist the hardiness of the blooms you would most like to use. They should be able to recommend a similar alternative should your first choice be prone to premature drooping, or behaves temperamentally when it comes to changes in weather conditions.

### Wreaths

Not just for Christmas. A wreath can be created from any seasonal flower or foliage and they look beautiful hung on a door as a really 'wow' entrance feature, to decorate your table plan, or at the top of the aisle.

Mini wreaths are also a lovely addition to wedding breakfast table décor when used as a method of displaying guests' name cards or as a napkin ring. Pegged up on string or ribbon, mini wreaths also make for a botanical alternative to fabric flag bunting.

Opt for bold, blowsy blooms if you want to make the ultimate *Midsummer Night's Dream*-esque style statement or, alternatively, a subtle circlet of greenery and delicate flower heads such as wax flower or daisies is both feminine and timeless.

I'm also a huge fan of the floral cuff, especially for bridesmaids, in place of a more traditional corsage or pomander. Ask your florist about adding your chosen florals to wire and wrapping it around your wrist; the effect is undeniably beautiful.

For the groom and groomsmen, the boutonnière, or buttonhole, is the traditional floral accessory of choice. Select flowers that you have chosen for your bouquet or general floral décor to tie everything together flawlessly. Alternatively, a floral print handkerchief in a jacket pocket is a befitting and non-perishable alternative.

# Choosing your Wedding Florist

As with any supplier, their availability for your wedding date is key. I'm the first person to tell you that it is absolutely possible to plan a wedding in a short time frame, but this may mean compromising on your supplier choice.

After you have discovered a florist whose designs you admire, I would advise requesting to view as much of their portfolio as possible. Their overall style, and whether their floral design inspires you, is important in determining if you feel confident that they will be able to deliver your overall vision. I would also suggest reading reviews from previous clients in order to gauge how passionate they are about their work – most professional florists will include these on their website.

An important piece of advice is to be very open and honest about your proposed spend. Share your ideas and examples of the bouquets, centrepieces and general floral décor that you love so that your florist is able to confirm whether your requirements are feasible within the confines of your budget. There may be varieties of flower that are very similar to your favourites but are considerably less costly due to being in season during the month of your big day, and a good florist will always suggest equally beautiful substitutions where appropriate.

If your florist has worked at your chosen wedding venue before then this may be a benefit, as they will be very familiar with the surroundings and what kind of floral décor has been designed in the past. You may also want to confirm what kinds of vases and props they have available to hire for the day, and whether there are extra charges associated with these, or if you will need to source certain items yourself. If you envisage a rustic display of crates and urns overflowing with blooms, for example, there is no denying this arrangement would be more straightforward if your florist was able to directly supply, or at least source, the aforementioned crates and urns.

It is important to clarify with your florist what tasks they are willing to carry out on the morning of your wedding as well as throughout the day, and how much time they have allocated from initial arrival. Florists will not necessarily be on hand to move arrangements from room to room later on in the afternoon, particularly if they have more than one wedding booked that day. This would ultimately be the responsibility of the staff at your venue. You will need to ask your florist what time they require access to the venue to set up your floral décor and when they will deliver your bouquets; these times will then need to be discussed and confirmed.

# Questions to ask your Wedding Florist

### Logistics

- Are you available on my wedding date? (This may seem obvious, but it's important to find this out before booking a consultation.)
- Will you have any other weddings on the same day?
- Will you personally be making up and delivering my florals or will it be a member of your team?
- Do you deliver bouquets/buttonholes or do we need to collect from you on the morning of the wedding?
- Do you set out all the flowers at the ceremony and reception venue yourself or will this be left to the venue staff?
- When do I need to make final flower choices?

### Vision and style

- Based on my ideas and venue, what arrangements do you suggest would work well?
- Which flowers would you suggest I choose based on my preferred colours, style and season?
- Can you show me examples of your floral creations similar to my proposed style?
- Have you worked at the ceremony/reception venue before? If not, would you visit the venue beforehand with us?

### Cost and practicalities

- Can you work within my budget? Are you able to suggest alternatives that are perhaps better value but equally as beautiful?
- Do you have a minimum budget that we have to spend, and does this include hiring vases, candleholders and other props?
- Do you offer wedding packages or is everything completely bespoke and tailor-made for each wedding?
- How do I secure your services for my wedding day? What deposit is needed?
- Will you provide an itemised proposal and quote with everything we have discussed?
- Will the delivery charges, travel, set-up and break-down charges be included in your quote?
- If I want you and your team to stay on site and move arrangements after the ceremony are you able to offer this service, and how much would this cost?
- When is the final payment due?

CHAPTER EIGHT

# DÉCOR

# Décor

**Much like attempting to include even a small percentage of the vast array of wedding gown designs available within this book, trying to highlight every item of décor would be nigh on impossible. There are infinite styling ideas for your big day, many of which I'm sure even I don't know about yet. And some that you will simply conceive yourself to create truly one-of-a-kind concepts.**

Essentially, everything you include in your wedding is decorative, from your florals to your paper goods to what you wear. Your personal choices all come together to create your bespoke wedding style – but of course there are many wonderful extras you can incorporate which can enhance the overall look and feel to, say, elegant and refined, or outright dazzling and spectacular.

Some ideas are infinitely easier and more straightforward than others, and there can be a significant difference in cost depending on which ideas you choose to incorporate and the quantities of decorations you decide to invest in. If you know what you want but believe you would benefit from a professional to assist you in the execution, or if you simply don't know where to start, an experienced wedding stylist could be a useful addition to your supplier contingent. There is obviously a cost associated with this option but you will be able to discuss an overall décor allocation budget with your stylist, which will also include their respective fee.

If it's been your lifelong dream to craft, make, purchase and create absolutely everything to do with your special day but you are having difficulty knowing where to start, we have our ultimate 'finding your personal style' advice on page 142. Alternatively, continue to devour this chapter and steal as many ideas as your heart desires.

# Paper Goods

I am a bona fide stationery geek. I love nothing more than a new notepad and the prospect of shopping for pretty and thoughtful greetings cards. Receiving a wedding invitation is therefore an absolute joy to behold; I am in equal parts thrilled at the prospect of attending a wonderful event and fascinated by the first glimpse of what style of affair I am going to experience. For me, a wedding invitation really sets the tone and starts to build the anticipation of the big day.

As with any element of your celebration, paper goods can vary from affordable to super luxe, all depending on the style, material, the quantities required and your budget allocation. It will come as no surprise that perhaps compared to most, I dedicated a healthy portion of our overall spend to creating the stationery suite of my dreams. I enjoyed the whole process immensely and was incredibly pleased with the final results.

As I said. Geek.

On the subject of stationery suite, traditionally a wedding will include at least one, some or all of the following items that collectively form the series of paper goods personalised to your wedding day:

## The 'Suite'

### Save-the-date

These are usually sent as soon as you have booked your venue, to ensure guests allocate that day for your wedding, giving you more time to decide on your final invitation design. Not everyone sends a save-the-date; my husband and I chose to because our wedding was planned within a fairly short time frame and we wanted to give our friends and family the best possible opportunity to be able to attend.

A save-the-date needs to include your names, the date of your wedding and your chosen venue details.

### The invitation

Invitations are typically sent three to four months prior to the date of your wedding, as with everyone leading busy lives it's wise to endeavour to secure the attendance of those you wish to celebrate your special day with as soon as you possibly can.

### Your invitation needs to include:

- Your names and/or the names of your parents if they are to be highlighted as hosts.
- Your venue name and location.
- Start and finish times.
- Instructions on how and where to RSVP, and the deadline to do so.

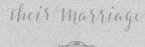

**Optional and additionally useful Information:**

- A map/directions to your venue location.

- Dress code details.

- Gift list details.

- A request for any dietary requirements.

- Recommendations for hotels within a reasonable distance from your venue should you expect some guests to stay overnight.

- A request for invitees' favourite songs to assist in compiling your ultimate wedding playlist.

### The Order of the Day

Often handed out when guests arrive at your venue, or written up on a large printed board, the Order of the Day details the running order of events during your celebration, usually beginning with the ceremony and finishing with what time the reception comes to a close. As a guest I think it's useful to know what the main aspects of the day are, such as the wedding breakfast, where they are occurring, and at what time.

### The Order of Service/Ceremony

Usually distributed by members of the wedding party as you arrive at the ceremony or placed on chairs within the room where your ceremony is being held, an Order of Service/Ceremony outlines exactly that – the details of your service/ceremony, including the entrance of the bride, any readings and who is reading them, processional and recessional music (if guest participation is required for any other music during the service/ceremony then lyrics may be included), and the signing of the register.

We decided to have an Order of the Day, which essentially also included our Order of Service within the ceremony details, thus we only needed to design and print one piece of stationery.

### Menus

Some couples choose to print a menu for every place setting and include it as a decorative statement within the table décor. Alternatively, one per table is more than adequate and is considerably more cost-effective.

### Guest place names

Traditionally each guest's name is placed at their allocated seat at the wedding breakfast table, the guests having been directed to their designated tables via the table plan (please see page 156 for further details). I recently attended a wedding where I was allocated a table number but essentially guests could sit where they pleased on that particular table. I can't say it made the least bit of difference to me personally, and as per the menu above, the fewer items required for materials and printing, the less you need to spend.

### Thank-you cards

If you want to tangibly create a final farewell to the celebrations of your nuptials, then a personalised thank-you card is a thoughtful touch for those who made the effort to attend your wedding and contributed to your gift list.

Before you conclude that any, or all, of the items that contribute to a stationery suite have to match in some way, then please don't. I love it when they do – it brings a certain style cohesion to the day just as your choice of flowers or general décor does. But there are no rules.

## Using a professional

You may want to create some items yourself, such as a decorative statement Order of the Day that you place in an obvious area for all of your guests to read, rather than supplying one per person, whilst leaving the rest to a professional and experienced designer, for example.

With regard to finding the perfect stationery supplier for you, it will be fairly clear from the details of their portfolio what their predominant style is, and whether you feel they are the right fit to create the type of paper goods you have in mind. Stationery is usually text- or illustration-led, or a combination of both. The quality, finish and colour of the stock that you choose to have your stationery made from will have a fundamental effect on the overall look, as well as on the cost. In terms of print, the traditional letterpress technique is beautiful, but is often considerably more expensive than regular digital printing.

You may wish to add statement foiling, embossing, ribbon or fabric to create texture and personal touches, but please bear in mind that all of these additions will incur extra cost. It is wise to discuss your budget with your stationery supplier at the very start of the design process so that they can meet your expectations and make alternative suggestions should they be required.

I would advise asking for samples where available so that you can get a real feel for the products you are considering making an investment in. What might appear dazzling online may not quite have the wow factor you envisaged once physically present on your kitchen counter.

In terms of actual design then the world's your creative oyster. If you find yourself overwhelmed with ideas and options, then confirming an elegant font is a good place to start. Your designer will be able to assist with making your desires a reality, or present a series of appealing concepts that you can choose from. Any information you can supply with regard to colour palette or other already confirmed décor details will also undoubtedly prove useful. Please see our recommended supplier list on pages 208–213 for some talented paper goods designers and makers.

## Do it yourself

Of course you can purchase wedding stationery off-the-peg, make an entire suite yourself should you have the means and ability to do so, or buy a design and then have it printed on a stock of your own choosing. With the ever popular and consistent growth in social media platforms, there is also a wealth of options for you to send communications virtually in the form of a wedding website, or via email.

I'm firmly in camp 'print-is-king', but there is no denying the affordability and ease of sending invitations and information across the World Wide Web.

# General Décor

### Floral alternatives

Flowers are an extremely popular choice as feature décor for a wedding and you can find out everything you need to know about beauteous blooms throughout our flowers chapter, which begins on page 110. If, however, you are not a lover of anything with petals then please do not stress, we have an abundance of alternatives for you to consider. My sister doesn't really like anything overtly floral, and even though I do sometimes wonder if we are in fact related, I can more than appreciate the exquisitely styled affairs that have graced the pages of the blog where the couple simply didn't want to include flowers of any kind. Anywhere. At all.

### Fruit

As well as being delicious, fruit can make *excellent* décor. Apples spilling out of baskets, peaches piled up as a table centre, or a pear place setting are all striking and effective ideas, and nothing says summer like decadent bowls of raspberries, cherries and strawberries – they add the perfect finishing touch to any dessert table or help-yourself punch bar.

Although I'm not entirely sure what one might do to make a bunch of bananas appear enticing, anything is possible, and most tropical fruits can look absolutely amazing. I've witnessed the most covetable glitter-coated pineapples combined with a palette of coral, orange and red to create a truly magnificent triumph of colour and fun.

For an atmospheric autumnal wedding no one can deny the appeal of stacked pumpkins combined with large pillar candles; they make a real style statement when used to decorate a main entrance or winding staircase. Pine cones and fallen leaves are equally eye-catching, and also practically free, should you find them in your own backyard. It's perhaps wise to request permission before you go on a foraging expedition in your neighbour's garden though. Obviously.

I'm also a huge fan of feathers; they add texture and interest to everything from boutonnières to bouquets to stationery. Please do take a peek at page 193 for how feathers were used to create the most magnificent headpiece.

### Ribbons

If you have read our bouquet section in the previous chapter then you will already be aware that a beautiful ribbon can add the final flourish to a bundle of blooms and potentially tie in with your colour theme, should you choose to incorporate one. The same goes for tying thin strips around napkins or cutlery at your wedding breakfast table.

Ribbons also look very pretty tied to the back of chairs: simply knot them and let them drape – varying lengths look chic, as does a subtle ombré effect. I also love ribbons as an alternative to traditional flag bunting; bound to a long piece of string or robe they can make a reasonably easy, yet incredibly charming, backdrop to the top of the aisle during your ceremony, your reception location or really anywhere you fancy for that matter.

# Tableware

Your venue will supply their own crockery and glassware; the style is usually plain and unobtrusive and will therefore blend in with your selected floral displays and overall styling choices. However, there are various companies that offer alternative tableware hire should you wish to make more of a statement with your actual plates and glasses. You could also scour flea markets, car boot sales and second-hand stores for original pieces – admittedly this may result in a rather mis-matched approach but I'm quite partial to a vintage enamelled flowery plate combined with an elegant crystal etched champagne flute.

Go one step further and consider your colour palette when choosing non-standard cutlery and serving ware. For example, copper accents work really well with foliage and all-white florals, whereas gold is particularly cohesive when paired with shades of peach, pink and coral. If you are organising a festival style affair then anything tin or galvanised is perfect. Of course, anything goes – and there are all sorts of ways in which you can update the standard tableware set-up, from simple place setting additions such as lace edged serviettes or jaunty coasters, to a complete vintage tea set.

Tablecloths and runners are also a super and straightforward way to update the overall look: think anything from simplistic rustic hessian to a full-on velvet and sequin drape.

# The Table Plan

Your table plan is an area where you can really go to town on the design. Often viewed as a very practical piece of décor (which of course it is, albeit often a pain in the proverbial backside when trying to decide on who sits where) it is actually one of the only pieces of decoration you can guarantee your guests will look at in detail on the day.

The options are endless. I've witnessed everything from a full-on apothecary display where guests are encouraged to take their very own medicine bottle complete with a single-stem flower that directs them to the correct table, to a simple display of hanging twine with cards to represent each table pegged to it and interspersed with blooms. Both were equally pretty.

One of the most popular ideas is to tie your table plan in with the rest of your stationery suite – your chosen paper goods designer, if you're using one, will have a wealth of ideas that they will share with you.

Other timeless and relatively simple ideas include a window pane or mirror paired with flowers of your choice and the table numbers and guest names simply written directly onto it in paint or chalk pen; a chalkboard is another classic option, as is a world map with your guests' names pinned to a table named after your favourite holiday destinations. I'm also fond of ornate frames with either the table numbers and names displayed on paper or card in one large frame, or a section of smaller-sized frames adhered to a board and placed on an easel.

Your table plan is an area where you can really let your creativity run wild in terms of inventing something original. I'm actually jealous that you get to create yours – I have LOADS of imaginative ideas, now that my own has been and gone for some years now. Hindsight and all that.

# Lighting

I'll be honest, lighting wasn't something I gave a second thought to for my own wedding day. I knew I wanted candlelight as the evening drew in, and that was provided by my venue in the form of various candelabras surrounded by hydrangea wreaths that I chose as my table centres.

Candlelight is *very* romantic and candles themselves make for excellent décor; there is a multitude of sizes, shades and even scents to choose from. I love the giant pillar variety for a touch of fairytale, especially when displayed in large hurricane lanterns, and tea lights are a budget-friendly way of adding a subtle twinkle throughout your venue. If it is romance you are after then fairy lights are another effective and accessible option: drape over table plans or use to change up any decorative display for the evening.

Festoon lighting is extraordinarily magical, and equally impressive when used indoors or outside; you can purchase smaller numbers of bulbs and cable lengths from most department stores or online. If you really want to incorporate a statement show-piece, there are event and lighting specialist companies worldwide who will supply as many lights as you desire, and work with you to create a truly spectacular installation.

If the lighting look you want to create is altogether more opulent and indulgent, then you could consider hiring chandeliers, or hanging multiples of luxury lampshades above any area of decorative interest.

# Signage

As well as your table plan, any additional signage makes for super wedding décor. Not only incredibly useful for directing your guests to the right place at the right time, your personal choices and unique combinations of materials and fonts can create truly bespoke one-of-a-kind designs. An Order of the Day sign displayed in a main focal point in the venue is indisputably useful, and as per your table plan, as mentioned on page 156, is likely to be viewed by most, if not all, of your guests.

Signs to describe what's on offer in terms of drinks and canapés, or which cocktails are available – complete with illustrations – are ever popular, as are welcome signs and specific

pointers to the various different locations of the day, from your ceremony to the dance floor, photo booth, and less glamorous (but absolutely necessary) ladies' and gentlemen's washrooms.

Signage isn't restricted to a rectangular board with written script at all; favourite words or names in giant lights are becoming increasingly popular, especially for evening décor, available to hire or even buy – the latter of which means you get a keepsake to take home as well! You could also consider floral fabric or felt lettering hung as alternative bunting to the back of chairs, or anywhere you require an eye-catching backdrop to your day.

# Interactive Décor

There's something very rewarding about decorations that are lovely to look at but also provide entertainment and interactive enjoyment for your nearest and dearest.

One of my favourites is a photo wall: collect pictures from various adventures you've experienced with your guests and put them on display for all to see. You can pin photos to a corkboard; use washi tape (low-tack masking tape) to fix them to a wooden palette; or, as per so many other décor options, peg them to string or ribbon and hang in an appropriately accessible and viewable space.

On the subject of photos, there is nothing quite as fun as a photo booth – hired or homemade – so that your guests can capture themselves and the hilarity of your special day – please find further detail in our reception section on page 23.

As we mention later in the beyond the wedding breakfast section on page 178, food and drink stations of your own creation can be a real focal point of the day. Adorn with flowers, fruits, ribbons and signage of your choice – they can be a real style statement and are always appreciated from an aesthetic perspective, as well as ensuring your favourite folk are constantly fed and watered.

Creating social 'areas' is becoming increasingly popular with couples, especially when their venue is very much focused on the available outdoor space. Rustic seating can easily be fashioned from hay bales covered with blankets, and if you require something a little more luxe, there are various furniture and prop hire companies worldwide who offer everything from very posh sofas to retro standard lamps. You can literally create your very own living room on the lawn.

CHAPTER NINE

# THE WEDDING
# BREAKFAST

# The Wedding Breakfast

**Not to be confused with a full English or a selection of Danish pastries, the wedding breakfast is the first meal you experience as a married couple, hence the reference to the first meal of the day, or breaking your 'fast'.**

Traditionally, this tends to be a sit-down, three-course affair, but as it is *your* day you can really dictate the service style and the details of your menu. Many couples are now choosing more creative options, from an afternoon tea or a relaxed and informal buffet where (unless your venue specifies otherwise) you can potentially request anything from Spanish tapas to an exotic Indonesian spread, should the skills of your caterer allow, to a feast of fresh Italian pizzas straight from authentic wood-fired ovens.

Preferred, or in-house, caterers of some wedding venues will usually have a selection of tried and tested dishes to choose from and will more often than not be willing to consider bespoke options should there be something in particular that you and your partner wish to incorporate on the menu. Please be aware there could be additional charges associated with anything that isn't offered as standard.

The final cost per head will be determined by the number of courses you choose for your guests and, of course, the type of food you include. Please make sure you are clear about what your venue or caterer charges for before confirming your selection, to avoid any surprise charges or unexpected added extras.

In terms of what you *should* choose for your menu, well, there isn't a right or wrong answer, but you can certainly start by considering dishes that you and your partner really enjoy. Please don't be swayed to incorporate what you feel are 'safe' options, or feel the need to pick something really original to try and create a cuisine that the majority of guests haven't experienced before. On the flip side, feel free to ignore entirely my explanation of the 'wedding breakfast', and take it literally – at any one of the real weddings I've personally attended, I've always secretly hoped to be offered a cinnamon croissant with a side of raspberry jam.

Choose food that you love to eat, that's the best advice of all.

# The Seating Plan

**Where should everyone sit? We know it's often not a straightforward task. Different families, different generations, friends who know each other and those who don't. It can really be a minefield with regard to trying to ensure all of your guests have a thoroughly enjoyable dining experience.**

I had a relatively small number of people to seat on the big day, 60 altogether – six round tables of between eight to ten guests and a 'top' table of six. My husband's parents are separated and both have re-married, so to negate a huge top table situation or potentially make the whole meal difficult or unfair, we chose to have me, my husband, the best man, my sister and my husband's sister (both bridesmaids) and my sister's partner sitting together. It worked out really well, and unless they were telling fibs, none of our parents minded in the least.

You don't have to have a top table at all; it is a long-standing tradition, but not one that is necessarily expected or makes the least bit of difference to your, or anyone else's, enjoyment of the day. An increasingly popular alternative is the 'sweetheart' table, just for you and your partner as newly weds, surveying a room full of your favourite folk. I think this is a wonderful compromise, and incredibly romantic.

Although round tables that seat between eight and ten guests seem to remain as the most popular choice, some venues offer long trestle designs instead of, or as well as, the circular options. And if you are hiring your wedding breakfast furniture from an external supplier then you may have the option to mix and match styles and create a really unique set-up.

In terms of where to begin, regardless of the shape of the tables you choose, you will ultimately need a full list of confirmed guests. Once you have all of your RSVPs ticked off, I would recommend writing each name on a small piece of paper and physically laying out your proposed seating plan – moving and switching around your little paper guests until you are satisfied with the outcome. From experience, the majority of couples endeavour to seat guests on the same table or close to at least a few other people they know reasonably well, to achieve a balance of everyone feeling comfortable and mixing a few groups up.

Before we were married, my husband and I once went to a wedding where although we were placed together at the wedding breakfast, we didn't know a soul on our allocated table, and it turned out no one else knew each other either. After a few minutes of polite conversation revolving around our respective relationship to the bride and groom, the wine flowed and we had one of the most hilarious evenings ever. Meeting new people can be heaps of fun, and by the very nature of being a guest at a wedding, you all automatically share a common interest – the couple getting married – so if the seating is giving you sleepless nights, don't be afraid to throw caution to the wind and try something a little bit different.

It is nigh on impossible to create what you might perceive as the 'perfect' seating plan,

and of course the more invitees the more complicated the task can often be. My advice would be to try to not let it worry you to the point it takes up valuable time that you could dedicate to the more fun aspects of your wedding breakfast organisation, such as designing the actual tangible seating plan itself. You may want to keep things very simple with a statement chalkboard design or an elegant printed plan in keeping with your suite of paper goods. Or maybe something a little more decorative, incorporating floral elements and a specific colour palette. We have a selection of styles and ideas to share with you within this section, which we hope are inspirational but by no means definitive; please do also refer to the previous chapter on décor, which will offer even more creativity.

# What's on the Table?

It may seem obvious initially, but in reality we hear from couples time and time again who haven't considered exactly how many items will need to be set on a standard round wedding breakfast table. There are actually multiple pieces used for dining, which can leave limited room for extras, such as stationery and favours, to include with each place setting. In direct contrast, the space in the middle of the table is often larger than anticipated, resulting in couples becoming concerned that their décor will seem lost and not have the impact they desire.

We have included a basic demonstration of a standard round wedding breakfast table set for eight guests, which we hope will give you an indication of scale and space and assist in helping you to plan your own table set-up accordingly.

1  Centrepiece

2  Favour and name card

3  Dinner plate

4  Side plate

5  Red wine glass

6  White wine glass

7  Champagne flute

8  Tumbler

9  Napkin

# Desserts

A WHOLE section dedicated to cake and various other delectable desserts? Yes, the rumours are true, I do have a penchant for a generous slice of Victoria sponge and every available shade of fondant fancy. I'm also a firm believer that, when it comes to your wedding, if you can find a way to make as many of your favourite things as multi-purpose as possible then go for it, as it will inevitably help the budget to go further.

Couples often still choose the tradition of serving a single wedding cake after the wedding breakfast, of which there are now a plethora of wonderful designs and ideas to consider. However, an increasingly popular alternative (or addition, we're not here to judge) is to present an entire dessert display, where guests can admire (and later tuck into) an array of after-dinner treats. Styled with props and floral accents to suit a theme, a table stacked with enviable delights makes for the perfect piece of statement décor with a purpose.

However, I'm not suggesting for one minute that you should invest in multiple high-end baked goods to create your display: one of the most memorable examples I have seen was a collection of French tarts from a local supermarket, complete with DIY signage and sweet bud vases filled with gorgeous greenery. Simple and budget-friendly, yet ever so effective.

If you're keen to include your friends and family in your wedding planning activities, one idea is to host a dessert 'bake off' and display the entries on the day for everyone to enjoy. The more variety the more fun, I say, and with a range of desserts there's bound to be something to suit everyone's tastes. Anything goes, from a tray of your aunty's best brownies to your best friend's lemon meringue pie. Delicious.

Of course a 'dessert' table does not have to relate to what we may associate with traditional puddings per se. How about a popcorn stand? Or a chest of drawers filled and topped with different flavoured cookies? Did someone say doughnut tower? Maybe even your own personal ice-cream van, or a retro pick 'n' mix bar so your guests can enjoy fizzy cola bottles, sherbet-filled flying saucers and pink shrimps with their glass of Sauvignon ... The possibilities are endless.

If savoury is the key to your most desired late night munchies, a 'cheese' cake may be the perfect variation on the theme for you. Imagine chunky round tiers of Cheddar, Stilton and Brie. Or any variety that takes your fancy for that matter. A nice touch could be to include cheeses from the local area, or a particular region you've been to on holiday, or ask members of your wedding party what their favourite cheese is as a way to include them. Decorate with colourful bunches of grapes, celery and your favourite biscuits and serve with a range of chutneys for the ultimate midnight snack.

If you do decide to create your own dessert masterpiece, please ensure you check with your venue first for any possible restrictions. Some venues will not allow any outside catering due to food hygiene and safety regulations, and some may permit some types of external food and drink to be brought in, but not others. From a money-saving perspective it is also worth asking your venue if they would consider serving your cake as part of your three-course wedding breakfast, thus potentially only having to cover the cost of a starter and main course for each guest.

# Beyond the Wedding Breakfast

**For some years, it has been commonplace for newlyweds to offer their guests food much later on in the evening, in addition to the wedding breakfast. A wedding can be more than a twelve-hour event and in order to ensure your guests have enough fuel to dance their socks off until the small hours, a late night snack is a very welcome treat.**

Your venue catering or independent caterer will be able to offer various options and, as with the main meal choice of the day, bespoke options can be made available upon request. Depending on the restrictions of your chosen venue, there is also the possibility of enlisting the services of a food truck; you can hire anything from an ice-cream cart to a fish and chip van. A modern take on meals on wheels, if you will.

As well as a feast to fuel your dancing feet, you may also be considering unique ways to serve drinks, both after the ceremony and post wedding breakfast. Much like food trucks, you can hire mobile vendors that specialise in your favourite beverages, from cider or beer to champagne and prosecco. Many couples even choose to create their *own* bar carts, not only to serve guests cocktails, but also as a source of entertainment and decoration.

This is another great way to allow your personalities to shine through. Over the years we've witnessed an array of amazing ideas on the blog, from more masculine gin and whiskey trolleys to a bubbly bar complete with decorative mini umbrellas and metallic straws. For those who don't necessarily fancy an alcoholic tipple, you could always consider a selection of juices complete with real fruit accompaniments, or a caffeine lover's alternative, such as a coffee cart with a selection of retro chocolate mints. I for one am quite partial to an After Eight, or two. And, if you offered up hot chocolate with whipped cream and marshmallows, particularly on a cold winter's night as the party winds down, all roaring fires and romantic ambience, well, that would probably be the greatest idea ever.

You may also be considering supplying your own wine and bubbles – please do check with your venue first that this is an option, and if it is, what the associated corkage charge might be. It can be a great way to stretch the budget *and* ensure you serve your preferred brands. However, sometimes the corkage added to the buying costs makes this option price prohibitive, so it's worthwhile doing your sums before making a decision.

On the subject of glass refilling, champagne
is the more obviously expensive option for post
ceremony celebrations and the more traditional
'toast' to the newly married couple. My venue
happened to offer cava, which worked for us as it
is considerably cheaper and – not that I am in any
way a connoisseur – actually a lot *nicer* in my opinion.

If the thought of considering yet more suppliers
sends you into a tail spin, and involving yourself
in anything remotely crafty bores you to tears
(it happens), then the vast majority of catering
services will have staffed options. All food and
drink, with the exception of initial choices on
*what* to provide, is simply someone else's concern.
Stand back and enjoy the moment whilst your
glass is refilled for you and you are offered
a selection of delicious comfort food canapés,
or perhaps even a bacon bap.

CHAPTER TEN

# THE TIMELESS WEDDING

# The Timeless Wedding

It's a question I hear time and time again: how do I make my wedding timeless?

Well, the answer to this question is that there is no straightforward answer. Terribly sorry about that. Trends come and go; fashions, colour combinations and themes fall in and out of favour on a regular basis, so there are no guarantees. And that's perfectly ok.

As long as at that moment in time you had the best day feasibly possible then that is all that matters. Besides, everyone's desires, likes and dislikes differ; you can't please everyone all of the time. And that's perfectly ok too.

As I mentioned in the introduction to this book, if you make your wedding truly a reflection of you as a couple, regardless of the budget, how long it takes you to plan or how many details you choose

or choose not to incorporate, those beautifully photographed moments of such a joy-filled occasion will stand the test of time.

When I think back to all of the thousands of unbelievably stunning affairs we have featured on Rock My Wedding since our launch in 2009, there are a particular few that are especially memorable. Not necessarily the most luxe, or because of the number of hours spent on DIY projects, nor because they exuded the kind of cool that makes you dizzy. But because they were pretty, and unique, and you could tell from every single moment captured that they were 100 per cent reflective of the couple themselves.

Completely and utterly timeless, in every single way.

# Eleanor & Kevin

PHOTOGRAPHY BY REBEKAH J. MURRAY PHOTOGRAPHY

Eleanor and Kevin met in London, currently live in Glasgow and were married in Leesburg, Virginia – a location near Eleanor's family. Their big day was a bona fide riot of colour and fun, incorporating stylish and decorative flourishes throughout their rustic barn backdrop and achieving their ambition for a 'carefree' aesthetic, tenfold.

Authentic, joyous and with friends and family at the heart, their wedding is as timeless as it is charming.

# Kate & Mark

PHOTOGRAPHY BY MCKINLEY RODGERS

Kate and Mark were married at the beautiful venue of Crear on the west coast of Scotland. Surrounded by such breathtaking views, their minimalist approach to décor paired with undone florals and a palette of pale hues worked perfectly with the dramatic landscape.

Whimsical lighting, the simplicity of the subtle use of feathers and Kate's determination to stay true to her everyday wardrobe (gold ankle boots and all) make this one of my favourite weddings of all time.

Contemporary, ethereal and unequivocally timeless.

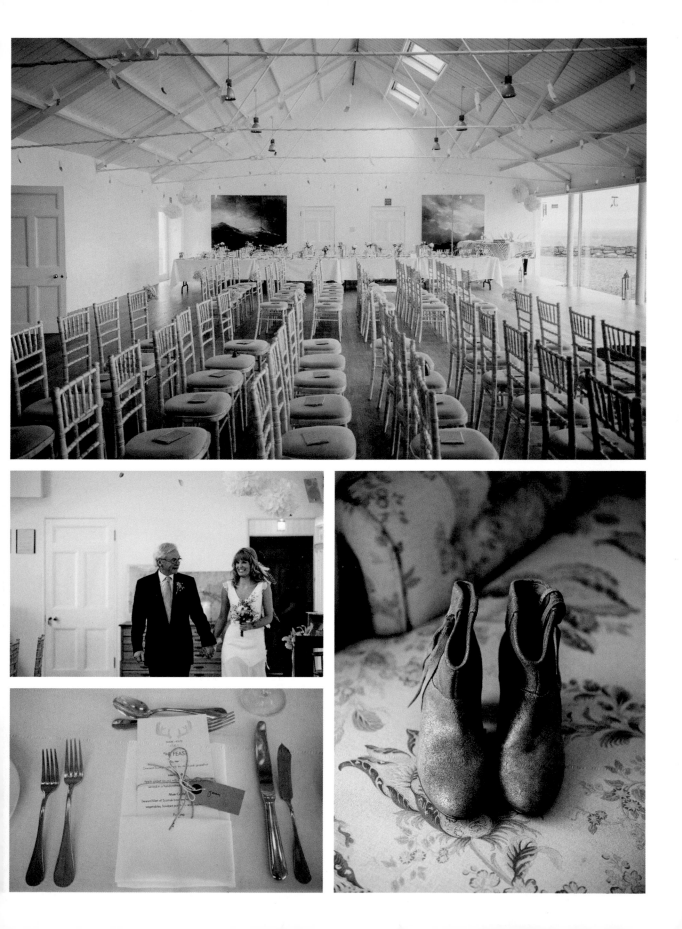

# Sophie & Simon

PHOTOGRAPHY BY DOMINIQUE BADER PHOTOGRAPHY

Sophie and Simon's Italian affair in the Tuscan countryside is the very epitome of elegance. From the sumptuous outdoor ceremony to the abundance of blowsy blooms and classic sartorial choices, every single element is as cohesive as it is visually impressive.

Each captured moment radiates sunshine, romance and joy, and what could possibly be more timeless than that?

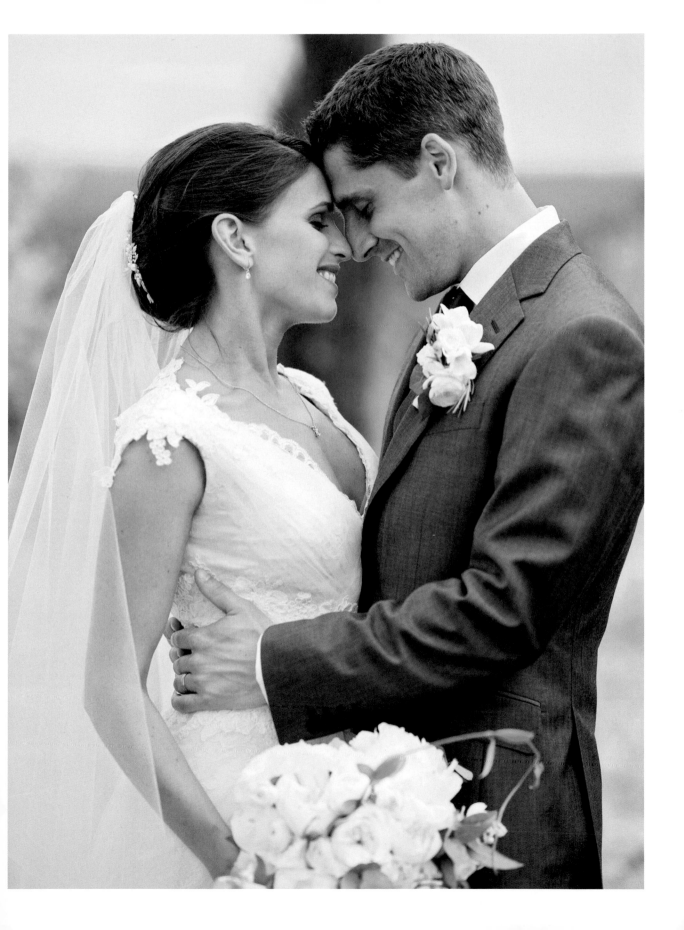

# Wedding Planner

Your monthly wedding to-do list

- Begin a Pinterest board
- Start compiling a binder or folder of things you like
- Work out your budget
- Choose your wedding party

## 12 MONTHS TO GO …

- Visit venues and check availability
- Book officiant/church and apply for your wedding licence
- Research suppliers
- Buy wedding insurance
- Write your guest list

## 11 MONTHS TO GO …

- Book a wedding planner if you'd like one
- Book your photographer and videographer
- Begin trying on dresses
- Research honeymoon options
- Look into accommodation for family and wedding party

## 9 MONTHS TO GO …

- Book a stationer (or consider what you want if you are making your own stationery)

- Confirm florist
- Order dress
- Taste cakes and book
- Send 'Save the Dates'
- Register for a gift list
- Book hair and make-up artists
- Look into groom's attire

## 6 MONTHS TO GO …

- Shop for bridesmaid dresses
- Confirm catering
- Book entertainment
- Arrange on-the-day transport for you and your wedding party

## 4 MONTHS TO GO …

- Buy underwear and shoes
- Confirm groom's attire
- Send your invitations
- Buy wedding rings
- Schedule dress fittings
- Schedule hair and make-up trials

### 8 WEEKS TO GO …

- Attend first dress fitting in *your* dress

- Finalise music choices and confirm with venue and band/musicians

- Confirm readings and Order of Service and send these to your officiant/vicar

- Meet with photographer for a catch-up or engagement shoot and confirm list of shots, if including formal shots on the day

- Chase anyone yet to RSVP

- Reconfirm with all vendors and suppliers

- Book hair appointments

### 3 WEEKS TO GO …

- Arrange a seating plan

- Write vows

- Book spa treatments

- Arrange a manicure

### 1 WEEK TO GO …

- Cut and colour hair

- Delegate small on-the-day tasks

- Pick up dress

- Get engagement ring cleaned

### THE NIGHT BEFORE

- Get an early night and have sweet dreams!

# Your Day Your Way

I sincerely hope you've found the contents of this book helpful and inspiring, and even if you've decided its only use has been to confirm everything you don't want to do, and you would rather elope, just the two of you, foregoing all wedding traditions, then that's absolutely fine with me.

Planning such a special occasion can be daunting, sometimes even intimidating, with such a vast array of choice and associated expectations. It's not unheard of to occasionally feel as though you want to lock yourself in a dark room with a bottle of red and a family sized assortment of biscuits because the pressure to have the 'perfect day' can become so overwhelming.

Been there, done that, got the empty confectionery wrappers to prove it.

If it does get to the stage where it all seems too much, and it's not actually particularly enjoyable, simply take a break and do something else. A weekend away can do wonders to revive your enthusiasm and decision-making prowess.

I want you to have one of the best days of your lives; I want you to have your day your way.

But most of all?

I want you to have a marriage that is even more beautiful than your wedding.

# Recommended Suppliers

Here are just a few of our favourite suppliers, you can search all of our recommended suppliers on The Love Lust List, thelovelustlist.co.uk

## FINE JEWELLERY

De Beers
debeers.co.uk

## VENUES

Almonry Barn (Somerset)
almonrybarn.co.uk

Aswanley (Scotland)
aswanley.com

Chiswell Street Dining Rooms (London)
chiswellstreetdining.com

Compton Verney (West Midlands)
comptonverney.org.uk

Cripps Barn (Cotswolds)
crippsbarn.com

Eleven Didsbury Park Hotel (North West)
eclectichotels.co.uk

Elmore Court (Cotswolds)
elmorecourt.com

Ever After (Devon)
lowergrenofen.co.uk

Hotel du Vin (National)
hotelduvin.com

Iscoyd Park (Shropshire)
iscoydpark.com

Nancarrow Farm (South West)
nancarrowfarm.co.uk

Notley Abbey (Buckinghamshire)
bijouweddingvenues.co.uk

Pennard House (Somerset)
pennardhouse.com

## PHOTOGRAPHERS

Anna from WE ARE // THE CLARKES (UK / Worldwide)
wearetheclarkes.com

Babb Photo (UK / Worldwide)
babbphoto.com

Chris Barber (UK / Worldwide)
chrisbarberphotography.co.uk

Claire Penn (UK / Worldwide)
clairepenn.com

Dominique Bader Photography (UK / Worldwide)
dominiquebader.com

Jonathan Ong (Australia / Worldwide)
jonathanong.com

McKinley Rodgers (UK / Worldwide)
mckinley-rodgers.com

Marshal Gray Photography (UK / Worldwide)
marshalgrayphotography.com

Mister Phill (UK / Worldwide)
misterphill.com

Paolo Ceritano (Italy/Worldwide)
paoloceritano.com

Peach & Jo Photography (UK/Worldwide)
peachandjophotography.co.uk

Rebekah J Murray Photography. (USA / Worldwide)
rebekahjmurray.com

Robbins Photographic (UK / Worldwide)
robbinsphotographic.com

S6 Photography (UK/Worldwide)
s6photography.co.uk

Sam Docker (UK / Worldwide)
samueldocker.co.uk

Sarah-Jane Ethan (UK/ Worldwide)
sarahjaneethan.co.uk

Source Images (UK / Worldwide)
sourceimages.co.uk

Touch Photography (UK / Worldwide)
touchphotography.co.uk

## VIDEOGRAPHERS

Ben Walton films
(UK/Worldwide)
benwaltonfilms.co.uk

Blooming Lovely
(UK/Worldwide)
bloominglovelyfilms.co.uk

Roost film Co (UK/Worldwide)
roostfilmco.com

Shoot Me Now films
(UK/Italy/Worldwide)
shootmenowfilms.com

Shutterbox films
(UK/Worldwide)
shutterboxfilms.co.uk

Silver Sixpence films
(UK/Wordwide)
silversixpencefilms.com

Simon from WE ARE // THE
CLARKES (UK/Worldwide)
wearetheclarkes.com

## FLORISTS

Emily Wisher (West Midlands)
emilywisherartisanflorist.co.uk

Floribunda Rose (London)
floribundarose.com

Grace & Thorn (London)
graceandthorn.com

Leafy Couture
(Yorkshire & Humberside)
leafycouture.co.uk

Mrs Umbels (East Midlands)
mrs-umbels.co.uk

Passion For Flowers
(West Midlands)
passionforflowers.net

Ruby & The Wolf (South West)
rubyandthewolf.com

The Country Flower Company
(East Midlands)
thecountryflowercompany.com

The Garden Gate Flower
Company (South West)
thegardengateflowercompany.
co.uk

Vanilla Rose (Scotland)
vanillarose.co.uk

Wild Orchid Designs (London)
wildorchidweddingflowers.co.uk

## DÉCOR & HIRE

Another Story Studio
anotherstorystudio.com

Anthology Vintage Hire
anthologyvintagehire.com

Doris Loves
dorisloves.co.uk

The Chalk Spot
thechalkspot.com

The Wedding Of My Dreams
theweddingofmydreams.co.uk

Virginias Vintage Hire
virginiasvintagehire.co.uk

## DRESS DESIGNERS

Amanda Wakeley
amandawakeley.com

Belle & Bunty
belleandbunty.co.uk

Catherine Deane
catherinedeane.com

Halfpenny London
halfpennylondon.com

Naomi Neoh
naomineoh.com

Rasbery Pavlova
rasberypavlova.com

Sassi Holford
sassiholford.com

Suzanne Neville
suzanneneville.com

Twobirds
twobirdsbridesmaid.co.uk

## SUITS

Cad & The Dandy
cadandthedandy.co.uk

Chester Barrie
chesterbarrie.co.uk

Jack Bunneys
jackbunneys.co.uk

## BOUTIQUES

Agape Bridal Boutique
(North West)
agapebridalboutique.com

Carina Baverstock (South West)
carinabcouture.com

Cicily Bridal (East Midlands)
cicilybridal.com

Coco & Kate (West Midlands)
cocoandkate.co.uk

Heart Aflutter Bridal (London)
heartaflutterbridal.co.uk

Mirror Mirror (London)
mirrormirror.uk.com

The Bridal Boutique
Warwickshire (West Midlands)
thebridalboutiquewarwickshire.
co.uk

The White Closet (North West)
thewhitecloset.co.uk

## ACCESSORIES

Britten Accessories For Brides
brittenweddings.com

De Beers
debeers.co.uk

Debbie Carlisle
dcbouquets.com

Harriet Wilde
harrietwilde.com

Liberty In Love
libertyinlove.co.uk

## MAKE-UP ARTISTS & HAIR STYLISTS

Beauty Call
beautycall.co.uk

Chloe MacCall
chloemccall.com

Harriet Rogers
hatmakeup.com

Lips & Locks
lipsandlocksuk.com

Make Up by Jodie
makeupbyjodie.co.uk

The Wedding Hair Company
weddinghaircompany.co.uk

## STATIONERY

Berin Made
berinmade.com

Bonny & Clyde
bonnyandclyde.co.uk

Gemma Milly
gemmamilly.com

Lola's Paperie
lolaspaperie.co.uk

Paper Knots
paperknots.co.uk

Pirrip Press
pirrippress.co.uk

Russet & Gray
russetandgray.co.uk

Studio Seed
studioseed.co.uk

Swoon at the Moon
swoonatthemoon.co.uk

The Uncommon Press
uncommonpress.co.uk

Tom Gautier
tomgautier.com

## CAKES

Bee's Bakery
beesbakery.co.uk

Buttercream & Dreams
buttercreamanddreams.com

Edible Essence Couture
Cake Company
edibleessencecakeart.com

Krispy Kreme
krispykreme.co.uk

The Confetti Cakery
theconfetticakery.co.uk

## CATERING

Baz & Fred
bazfred.com

Bubble Bros Ltd
bubblebros.co.uk

Cin Cin
cincin.co.uk

Jacaranda Catering
jacarandacatering.com

Kemp & Kemp
kempandkempcatering.co.uk

Pickle Shack
pickleshack.co.uk

The Wild Fork
thewildfork.co.uk

## ENTERTAINMENT

Alive Network
alivenetwork.com

Discowed
discowed.com

The Zoots
thezoots.com

Vintagebooth.me
vintagebooth.me

Warble Entertainment
warble-entertainment.com

Wedding Jam
weddingjam.co.uk

## GIFT LIST

The Wedding Shop
weddingshop.com

## MARQUEE & TIPI

Big Chief Tipis
bigchieftipis.com

Castle Yurts Ltd
castleyurts.co.uk

PapaKata
papakata.co.uk

The Little Top
thelittletop.co.uk

Will's Marquees
wills-marquees.co.uk

## PLANNING / STYLING

Duchess & Butler
duchessandbutler.com

Liz Linkleter Event Planning
& Design
lizlinkleter.com

Mark Niemierko
niemierko.com

Potcakes
potcakes.com

The Wedding Stylist
thewstylist.co.uk

Utterly Wow
utterlywow.co.uk

# Picture Credits

## PHOTOGRAPHY

Dominique Bader Photography: 19, 64, 81, 198, 199, 200, 201, 202, 203

Chris Barber Photography: 26, 30, 32, 53, 55, 57, 61, 85, 158

Anna Clarke from WE ARE // THE CLARKES: 3, 5, 6, 7, 11, 13, 14, 17, 21, 22, 23, 28, 29, 32, 39, 56, 59, 61, 65, 66, 69, 70, 72, 74, 75, 76, 77, 79, 82, 86, 89, 90, 91, 92, 95, 96, 99, 101, 103, 104, 105, 109, 110, 113, 114, 117, 118, 119, 129, 130, 133, 135, 138, 141, 143, 145, 147, 148, 152, 157, 160, 163, 164, 167, 169, 170, 171, 173, 175, 176, 177, 179, 180, 205, 207, 209, 210, 215, 221, 223

Adam Crohill: 30, 85, 107, 115, 120, 121, 122, 123, 124, 125, 126, 127, 224

Sam Docker: 29, 40, 41, 42, 65, 79, 152, 159, 161, 175

Rebekah J Murray Photography: 18, 49, 50, 57, 62, 64, 65, 119, 133, 151, 154, 155, 181, 186, 187, 188, 189, 190, 191

Jonathan Ong: 25, 33, 43, 119, 132

Claire Penn: 53

Robbins Photographic: 18, 29, 32, 35, 45, 47, 60, 79, 85, 88, 132, 133, 137, 185, 213

McKinley Rodgers: 30, 86, 106, 114, 129, 151, 152, 155, 161, 182, 192, 193, 194, 195, 196, 197

Source Images: 18, 26, 29, 53, 64

## VENUES

Almonry Barn: 39, 129, 138, 163, 167, 169, 171, 179, 207

Iscoyd Park: 3, 5, 6, 7, 11, 13, 21, 22, 23, 36, 56, 59, 66, 69, 70, 74, 75, 76, 77, 79, 89, 90, 91, 92, 99, 101, 103, 104, 105, 110, 113, 114, 117, 118, 119, 130, 133, 135, 141, 145, 147, 148, 157, 160, 164, 170, 173, 180, 209, 210, 215, 223

## FLOWERS

Karen Morgan from Passion For Flowers: 59, 74, 77, 79, 90, 91, 92, 101, 103, 110, 113, 114, 117, 118, 119, 122, 123, 129, 130, 133, 138, 141, 145, 147, 148, 157, 160, 163, 164, 167, 169, 170, 171, 173, 176, 177, 179, 180, 207, 215, 223

# Special Thanks

This book wouldn't have been possible without the creativity and dedication of a team of hugely talented experts whom I had the pleasure of working with.

Firstly, photographer Anna Clarke from WE ARE // THE CLARKES. She captured the vast majority of styled editorial throughout these pages and managed to make it look exactly how I envisaged it. If you haven't already secured a wedding photographer then you should probably enquire to see if she's available. She'll make you laugh until you cry whilst still making you look ridiculously beautiful.

Karen Morgan from Passion For Flowers followed us halfway around the country with her magnificent blooms and ability to whip up a floral storm in an unprecedented short amount of time. I swear she is actually Mary Poppins in disguise – her van plays host to a seemingly limitless supply of trinkets and decorative pieces from her daughter Gemma's wedding décor store – The Wedding Of My Dreams.

Phil Godsal from Iscoyd Park hosted us for a series of long weekends and let us run riot on his stunning estate, as well as assisting me greatly with the 'Questions to ask your Venue'. Iscoyd Park is not only breathtaking in its space, light and panoramic views, it is also one of the best organised venues in the UK, with on-site accommodation to rival some of the country's most luxurious hotels.

If it's a rustic yet chic barn backdrop you're after then you would be hard pushed to find a more perfect location than Almonry Barn in Somerset. The exterior is just as pretty as the interior, with an abundance of blossom trees and a romantic swing.

Sophie Derry who owns the fairytale boutique, Coco and Kate, not only let us borrow a delicious selection of froth and fancy in the way of every type and style of gown imaginable, she also bestowed upon us her extensive knowledge and dress fitting expertise. You need to arrange an appointment at her charming shop. It is a treasure trove of ethereal bridal wear and covetable accessories.

As well as Karen Morgan (aka Mary Poppins), Emily Wisher, Sarah Pike from Mrs Umbels Flowers and Jemma Gade from The Country Flower Company created the stunning seasonal bouquets that fill our Flowers chapter with colour, texture and endless possibilities. You should absolutely consider booking any one of these lovely green-fingered ladies for your special day.

Bonny and Clyde Design Studio supplied us with endless paper goods. They create stunning stationery and will turn your favourite ideas into a reality.

We borrowed an abundance of unique and magical props to style these pages and would like to thank Another Story Studio, Anthology Vintage Hire, The Wedding Of My Dreams and Virginia's Vintage Hire for driving miles and loaning us their wonderful wares. You too can borrow some of their pieces for your special day. All of the web addresses and contact details are in our recommended supplier section, on pages 208–213.

I would like to thank Pen & Cam from McKinley Rodgers, Jordan and Ines from Source Images, Lee Robbins from Robbins Photographic, Sam Docker, Chris Barber from Chris Barber Photography, Rebekah Murray from Rebekah J Murray Photography, Jonathan Ong and Dominique Bader from Dominique Bader Photography for allowing us to share their perfect images. These photographers are some of the very best.

I would like to thank our agent Bell Lomax Moreton for giving us the confidence to believe we could secure a book deal, and to Ebury Publishing for being a dream to work with. Ebury completely understand our brand's aesthetic and ethos and have enabled us to achieve the ultimate goal – our work in print. A special mention to our editor, Lydia Good, who is officially the Queen of piecing together thousands of ideas and, alongside our brilliant designer Jim Smith, evolving them into a cohesive and beautifully curated book.

Last but not least I would like to thank Adam Crohill, Charlotte 'Lottie' Manns, Lauren Coleman, Fern Godfrey, Lolly Gautier-Ollerenshaw, Becky Sappor, Laura Humphrey , Lorna Shaw and Lisa Bunton for constantly giving their all, and then some, into building and evolving the Rock My brand. It's a constantly crazy ride, and I couldn't think of a lovelier or more hilarious bunch to spend it with.

We believed we could, so we did.

# Index

...because we share them.

...a key to stories...

...reached out and...

...involved with life...

...you would never...

...alone. A truly

marriage is troubled

there can be no.

found to ensure a

...married life.

# About the Author

Charlotte O'Shea founded rockmywedding.co.uk in 2009.
Since then the brand has evolved into one of the most influential
in the wedding industry with over 1.2 million followers across
social media platforms, and hundreds of thousands of readers
visiting the blog every month. Interiors, fashion and beauty blog
rockmystyle.co.uk was launched in 2013, and rockmyfamily.co.uk,
a platform for parents on the joys and challenges of parenthood,
was launched in 2015.

Charlotte believes that every bride and groom should have
their wedding *their* way; that it's about the joy as much as the
pretty; and that love truly does conquer all. Charlotte lives in
Warwickshire with her husband James, their daughter Mabel
Rose, and a vast collection of floral tea dresses and ankle boots.